THE STICKS

A Profile of Essex County, New York

Also by Burton Bernstein

THE GROVE

THE LOST ART

THE STICKS

A Profile of Essex County, New York

BURTON BERNSTEIN

Drawings by Marcia Erickson

DODD, MEAD & COMPANY · NEW YORK

Portions of this book appeared originally in *The New Yorker*
under the title "North Country Luck"

ISBN: 0-396-06528-7
Library of Congress Catalog Card Number: 71-39651
Printed in the United States of America
by Vail-Ballou Press, Inc., Binghamton, N.Y.

To the good people of the North Country

THE STICKS

A Profile of Essex County, New York

DUE north of New York City, up the Hudson Valley past the undisciplined Westchester and Rockland sprawl, north beyond Peekskill, Newburgh, Poughkeepsie, Kingston, Albany–Troy–Schenectady, all reaching out to touch each other; then north still, toward the source of the narrowing, meandering Hudson, past the tiny congestions of Saratoga Springs and Glens Falls, past the splendor and honky-tonk of Lake George, lies the massive chunk of New York State known variously as the Adirondacks, the Great Northern Wilderness, the North Country, the Sticks. For millions of non-campers, non-skiers, non-hunters, and non-naturalists, the North Country is one of those regions that occasionally come to mind when one is thumbing through a *National Geographic* in a dentist's waiting room, or helping a child with his American-history home-

work, or trying to decipher a ballot question about some forest preserve in a poorly lit voting booth. And there are certain place names that ring a bell: Lake Placid, Ticonderoga, Whiteface Mountain, Schroon Lake, Ausable Chasm, Crown Point. Few people know exactly where these places are on the map, but many have heard of them. Where these places are—and where almost everything of significance in the North Country is to be found—is on an enormous tract of land, a kind of keystone of the whole area, called Essex County.

A road sign outside Elizabethtown, the county seat, bills Essex as "THE MOST INTERESTING COUNTY IN THE STATE," and while the local boosters will get a strong argument from their fellows to the south, they are not terribly far off the mark. The second-largest county in the state (St. Lawrence is the largest), Essex commands 1,823 square miles, or 1,166,720 acres—roughly the area of the entire state of Delaware. Almost all this territory is within the six-million-acre Adirondack Park, of which 2,246,000 acres belong to the Adirondack Forest Preserve, a constitutionally protected, state-administered expanse of perennial controversy. (The state actually owns only about forty-four per cent of the parkland in Essex County.) The whole eastern boundary of Essex County abuts on Lake Champlain, an inland sea that connects by rivers and canals to both the St. Lawrence and the Hudson. West of the shoreline are rich farmland and pleasing hills, and then, with awesome abruptness, the ragged mountains. The county contains the grandest of the Adirondacks, in-

cluding the highest mountain in New York State and one of the highest east of the Rockies—Mount Marcy, which rises 5,344 feet. For every peak there is at least one deep, clear tarn, feeding rocky rivers or streams that are set in some of the handsomest forests in the world. The county has rare-mineral deposits, good fishing and hunting grounds, tourist attractions, hiking trails and campsites, skiing centers, historical landmarks, Interstate 87 (the Northway), an Olympic bobsled run, and a stern but healthful climate. The air covering all this is pure and sweet and invigorating.

While Essex County seems to be blessed with the lion's share of North Country advantages, it is also cursed with an elephantine portion of North Country problems. There is some dispute about whether the Adirondack Mountains should be considered a part of the Appalachian range, which bumps its way down eastern North America from Quebec to Alabama; technically, most geologists hold that certain old rocks in the haphazard profusion of Adirondack rocks are more closely akin to those in the Laurentian system of Canada. Among sociologists and economists, however, there is general agreement that the Adirondacks are Appalachian indeed. The mountain people of both the Appalachians and the Adirondacks are, for the most part, descendants of early white settlers from the British Isles. They took to the difficult upland regions first as hunters and as timber cutters to clear the land, then as farmers when enough land was cleared, then as hunters and timber cutters again when the stony, re-

stricted farming failed, and, finally, as miners when the real worth of the mountains was discovered. Of these Appalachian–Adirondack pursuits, all have diminished to a bare survival level in the mid-twentieth century. Besides these economic dregs, there is a smattering of industry and, in a few lucky scenic spots, some tourism. But mostly there is grim rural poverty. Essex County, less than five hours by car from New York City, is, indeed, a classic example of this condition.

History hasn't always been kind to the county, but it has had more than ample opportunity; in fact, Essex County has probably had more history than any other county in the United States—certainly more bloody history. In the beginning, there was, of course, the Indian. But for an area whose Indian names and legends are as plentiful as the black flies in May, surprisingly few red men settled there permanently. As a result, little is known about the region's Indians before the first white man set his heavy foot in it. It has been accepted by historians—white historians, at any rate—that Algonquins and Hurons from north of the St. Lawrence and Mohawks of the original Iroquois Five Nations used the mountains, lakes, and rivers for hunting, fishing, and trapping. Game was varied and abundant, and an enterprising brave could take home enough meat to last his family through even a North Country winter. (Relics from temporary Indian campsites can still be found near the banks of rivers, where the Algonquins, particularly, liked to spend their nights.) Once the Indians had sufficient game, they would

haul the booty home to their villages, in the more hospitable and arable flatlands north, west, and south of the mountains, travelling by way of a majestic pass through the highest Adirondack peaks (still called, not unexpectedly, Indian Pass) or by canoe or sled (depending on the season) over what is now Lake Champlain. The Indians named the hundred-and-twenty-mile-long waterway "*Caniadere guarante,*" or "Lake that is gate of the country"; the Great Northern Wilderness was the Sticks even to the Indians. As the lake traffic grew, around the sixteenth century, a few Iroquois way stations sprouted along the western shore to handle the commerce, and these outposts caused rancor between the Iroquois and the Algonquins, heightening earlier ill will over hunting and fishing rights. A war was fought, and the Algonquins were badly beaten by the superior Iroquois. As legend has it, the victors taunted the vanquished with the Iroquoian epithet "*Rat-i-ron-taks,*" meaning "They who eat the bark of trees"—an oblique way of saying that the Algonquins were too weak to kill even game and so had to live on tree bark. The French later heard the phrase as "Adirondacs," and the British changed it even later to "Adirondacks." In name, anyway, the vanquished became the victors.

It's a nice story, but it's probably not true. J. N. B. Hewitt, of the Smithsonian Institution, has reasoned that the word originated with an obscure sixteenth-century Canadian Indian tribe and that it meant "They of the great rocks." The Iroquois picked it up and mistranslated

it to "They who eat the bark of trees," using the term to poke fun at inept hunters of any tribe who were forced to live on bark during rough winters. And, to make matters worse, a dictionary of Mohawk words compiled by Dutchmen in 1634 lists the word "*Aderondacke*," meaning "Frenchmen and Englishmen." One point is clear, however: the Adirondacks were not a tribe of Indians but a cursed human condition of the time. Many North Country people think the bark-eating curse is still relevant. In any case, whatever trials the Indians who frequented the area had had to put up with were nothing compared with their life from July 30, 1609, on. That was the day—eleven years before the Pilgrims landed at Plymouth Rock—that the first white man set foot in what is now Essex County.

The white man was Samuel de Champlain, an ambitious French explorer, who had been in Quebec, New France, for a year trying to revive interest in the flagging settlement there. He had heard rumors about the great wilderness to the south from the local Indians, and in the summer of 1609 he, two other Europeans, and sixty friendly Algonquins and Hurons went up the Sorel River (now the Richelieu) in twenty-four canoes to that long body of water he was so quick to name after himself. As Champlain neared the lake, he remarked in his journal, with some relief, that "these parts, though agreeable, are not inhabited by any Indians, in consequence of their wars." That was his impression from the canoe. He was to amend it when he came ashore, near the present-day

Crown Point—a flat peninsula almost touching the opposite, or Vermont, side of the lake. There he encountered a party of Iroquois from the Mohawk Nation, and, making no real attempt to communicate with them, he loaded his harquebus with four balls and fired point-blank, killing two chiefs right off. The rest of the Iroquois were easy prey for Champlain's companions. The explorer later wrote in his journal, "They lost courage, took to flight and abandoned the field and their fort, hiding themselves in the depths of the forest, whither pursuing them, I killed some others. Our savages also killed several of them and took ten or twelve prisoners. . . . The place where the battle was fought is in forty-three degrees some minutes latitude, and I named it Lake Champlain."

The Iroquois loathed the French and most Canadian Indians for decades thereafter, and at the end of the seventeenth century, when the British and the French were lining up allies for the endless bloody battles that were to follow up and down Essex County, the Iroquois threw in their lot with the British. The Algonquins and the Hurons sided with the French. The only real losers were the Indians.

No man in the North Country feels this loss with more bitterness today than Ray Fadden, the builder, curator, and lecturer-in-residence of the Six Nations Indian Museum, in the hamlet of Onchiota. Short, pug-nosed, alabaster-skinned, and with a shock of wavy gray hair, Fadden is mostly Scottish, but the blood in his veins he cares about is the blood of an Akwesasne, or St. Regis, Indian

ancestor, a member of one of the tribal remnants of the Mohawk Iroquois, who still have a reservation near Hogansburg, on the St. Lawrence River. Fadden, a prolific pamphleteer on Indian history and culture, signs his work "Aren Akweks," his Indian name, and he is equally proud of "Te-ha-ne-to-rens," his Iroquois longhouse name. Fadden said that when he "got fed up with the phony white version of Indian history" he accepted a job at the school on the Tuscarora Reservation and then at the St. Regis Reservation, instructing young Indians in their own culture. In 1935, he married a St. Regis woman, who is pure Indian. They have a son, John, who dresses in Indian garb, speaks perfect Iroquoian, is a graduate of the Rochester Institute of Technology, and, like his father, is a teacher. Together, the family runs the museum.

Fadden works doggedly on his museum with a sense of divine mission. He built it (in the style of a longhouse) from native logs and constructed model stockades, villages, and tepees on the grounds, and he is constantly cramming into the tight exhibition space more artifacts and wordy displays of explanation, history, and propaganda. As a driven Indianologist and a despairer of the white man, he will deliver three intense lectures, chain-smoking as he talks, on Indian civilization and suffering to even one visitor. "I have so much to say that I never really repeat," he told a friend not long ago, after one of his lectures. "Somebody has to clear the air of the lies and more lies the whites have been telling about us. What do the white so-called historians say? They say that the Iro-

quois had hardly any brains at all, that he was a base, warlike savage, that he had little regard for marriage, no culture or civilization, that his food was rotten and that he was unclean, that he degraded his women and children, and so on—until the wonderful European came and showed him the good life. Well, it's simply not true. Long before that murderer Champlain invaded this area, the Iroquois had a democratic civilization that should still be a model for the whites. The Iroquois had more freedoms than Americans do now. No sachem ever commanded; all decisions had to be unanimous. The sachem was elected by his clan and could be impeached by his clan. His son was just the same as any other brave. Why, Lieutenant Governor Cadwallader Colden, a colonial administrator of New York, wrote in 1747 that Iroquois chiefs were elected on the basis of their merit, because of their honesty and integrity, and that they were usually the poorest men in the nation—never keeping anything for themselves, but distributing all annuities and monies equally among the people. That was thirty years before the American Revolution. Now, where do you think the whites got the idea for equality, brotherhood, and democracy? Certainly not from Europe. As for being a cruel savage, the Iroquois never beat his wife or children, he cared for his old people, and he was generous to a fault—a fatal fault. When Henry Hudson came up to Albany on the *Half Moon*, just a couple of months after Champlain's landing here, Hudson repaid the Mahicans' kindnesses by getting them all drunk. The Dutch fur traders who fol-

lowed him cheated the Indians blind—six quarts of cheap rum for six beaver skins, when those skins went for incredible prices in Europe. The same was true of all the traders, soldiers, and settlers who followed, whether they were Dutch, French, or English. They would have died like babes in the wood without the Iroquois' help. We taught the puny European to dress light but warm in the winter, and to bathe properly, and to swim with the overhand stroke instead of the primitive breaststroke, and to breathe fresh air while sleeping, and to grow beans and corn, and a thousand other things. Baron Lahontan, one of the early French explorers, said of the Iroquois: ' 'Tis a great rarity to find any among them that are lame, hunch-back'd, blind or dumb. Their eyes are large and black, as well as their hair. Their teeth are white like ivory, and the breath that springs from their mouth in expiration is as pure as the air that they suck in.' The first Jesuit priest who tried to convert the so-called heathen around here, Father Pierre Biard in 1611, even he had to admit that if it wasn't for the kindness and hospitality of the Indians he would have died during his first winter. But a lot of French Jesuits just gave up on converting the heathens and sent soldiers in to wipe them out. That was how the Indian was rewarded—with death, robbery, rum, cheating, and lies."

Fadden stamped out his cigarette. "The lies," he said. "Do you know that scalping, skinning alive, and burning at the stake were European barbarian inventions, forced on Indian mercenaries? When the Indian was left to him-

self, he fought fair, for what was his—not just to torture and kill. The white historian can't even get the story straight on the fight between the Algonquins and the Iroquois. They had no war until the whites arrived. They had a few squabbles over hunting rights and the use of Lake Champlain, maybe, but no war. Wampum-belt symbols here in the museum show that the two groups considered themselves brothers, and still do. We St. Regis have Algonquin blood in us. So the supposedly humiliated and defeated Algonquins of the Adirondacks did not have to eat tree bark to survive. The truth is that Indians of all tribes who used the Adirondack area liked to flavor their food with ground-up dried bark. They used it like pepper. That's how the Adirondacks got their name."

Fadden's son John broke into the lecture, giving his father the chance to find a fresh pack of cigarettes. "What we're trying to do here is to educate both the Indians and the whites, in our small way," John said. "Fortunately for us, there's a surge of interest now in things Indian, and there's a kind of Indian nationalism, like black nationalism, which we feel very close to. More and more people on our reservation, and Iroquois all over New York and Canada, are leaving Christianity and going back to Indian religion. They come up to the reservation in the summers for vacations and they get interested. We like the feeling of being together. It's not segregation for us. It's our land. At Rochester, when other students found out I was an Indian, they wanted to know everything about what it was like. There was some kidding—just like

here in Onchiota, with kids going 'wa-wa-wa' when they pass the museum on their bikes—but most whites are finally trying to understand us. A lot of it is guilt, of course. When I was growing up on the reservation, I ran into some discrimination in the town of Fort Covington. The white kids would beat me up for being a redskin, mainly because our parents, on the reservation, didn't have to pay taxes and their parents, in Fort Covington, did. But I got over it. I married an Indian girl, and now I want to live like my father. I just wish he wouldn't work so hard."

Fadden returned with his cigarettes, and said, "You know, I've heard many white folks from around here boasting about how they had an Indian great-grandmother or great-uncle, or something. Mostly hogwash, or maybe wishful thinking. But still it's interesting that they say so now. And there *is* a certain look in some faces. Who knows?"

The Dutch fur traders enjoyed their magnificent beaver swindle of the Iroquois until the mid-seventeenth century, when Charles II ceded most of colonized America to his brother James, Duke of York. Besides the beaver spoils in the North Country, the British inherited the loyalty of the Iroquois and, consequently, the enmity of the Iroquois to the French. This hatred, beginning with the first meeting of the Mohawks with Champlain, reached a new high in 1642, when a Jesuit missionary, Father Isaac Jogues, was captured by Mohawks who tore his hair out, gnawed his hands, and then axed him to

death. But the soldiers and settlers of New France were not discouraged; they continued to make military expeditions of varying success south along Lake Champlain, much to the concern of the British colonists who were beginning to realize the full strategic and economic value of the Great Northern Wilderness between Quebec and Albany. At one point, the Colonial Assembly of New York went so far as to pass a law imposing the death penalty on every Jesuit caught in its territory. Father Jogues was, in a sense, as much a victim of the British as of the Iroquois. Even an illiterate dirt farmer could tell from just a glance at the crude maps of the day that control of the Champlain "highway" was control of the whole region. A convention of delegates from Massachusetts, Connecticut, and New York was held in 1690 to contrive a plan to beat the French at their own real-estate game. Land forces were sent to Lake Champlain, but the expedition was abandoned when supplies and esprit de corps quickly ran out. It was also an expensive venture for the struggling colonists, and they had to bide their time for a while. A few other minor but gory expeditions against the French, led by various Schuylers, accomplished little except some indiscriminate scalping.

The Treaty of Ryswick was signed in 1697, and while it established a shaky peace between the French and English by having each party return to its original possessions, it did not include the Indians loyal to either side. The Iroquois continued to hold the North Country, to all intents and purposes, and continued to be a thorn in the

side of the French. The treaty notwithstanding, both British and French soldiers inched towards each other along the Champlain Valley, with the strategic spits of land known as Crown Point and Ticonderoga as the main prizes. By 1731, the French could stand the suspense no longer. A crack military force swooped south on Lake Champlain and occupied Crown Point, where an impressive structure, Fort St. Frédéric, was erected. A colony of fifteen hundred settlers soon followed, establishing themselves on the fertile land around the fort and becoming one of the more stable communities in the New World. This was all made possible by the largesse of Louis XV, who promised his soldiers grants of land, provisions, agricultural tools, and one cow each after their short military service was completed. The royal land grants covered a good deal of what is now Essex County. So secure and prosperous was the Crown Point colony that Peter Kalm, a member of the Swedish Royal Academy of Sciences, visited it in 1749 and wrote: "I found the people of distinction had here a much greater taste for natural history and other learning than in the English colonies." The thick gray limestone walls of Fort St. Frédéric also provided an ideal base for French raids on British settlements to the south, the ferocity of which at last tweaked the torpid English. And when the French began the construction of Fort Carillon at Ticonderoga in 1754, even closer to the British heartland, the colonial authorities became truly indignant. They raised an army of militia and volunteers from several colonies, all under the command of Sir Wil-

liam Johnson, to march against the French at Ticonderoga. Meanwhile, the French sent Baron de Dieskau and six battalions of regulars to bolster the Champlain defenses. The Indians stood by their usual alliances, and the French and Indian War—the American version of Europe's Seven Years' War—was officially declared.

The two armies, the strongest the New World had ever seen, met not at Ticonderoga or Crown Point but at the head of what Father Jogues called Lac du St. Sacrément, which Sir William Johnson hastily renamed Lake George in honor of his king, George II. Both Johnson and Dieskau were wounded early on at Lake George and casualties were high on both sides, but the British colonists seemed to have more fight in them. They ultimately routed the French, took Dieskau prisoner, captured a great deal of war booty, but, because of the arrogant Johnson's timidity, they allowed the French to escape back to Fort Carillon. Instead of pressing his advantage, Johnson casually took time out to have Fort William Henry constructed on Lake George, and to accept a baronetcy and an award of five thousand pounds from the delighted, if impecunious, colonists. While the British relaxed, the French strengthened their Lake Champlain forts, but this time under the talented leadership of the Marquis de Montcalm, who had replaced Dieskau as commander of the forces of New France.

At first, the ineffectual and apathetic British officers didn't realize the full import of the change in command; for the time being, they were content to leave the active

warfare to the colonists' own devices. Their own devices were the Rangers—Rogers, Stark, Prescott, Putnam, Pomeroy, and companies—brutish locals who had studied carefully the fighting techniques of the Indians and copied the moccasin guerrilla warfare with devastating results, often against their very instructors. Montcalm, meanwhile, had thoroughly ingratiated himself with his Indians and used them for scouting and guerrilla operations. He grew increasingly confident of himself and his forces of about five thousand Frenchmen and sixteen hundred Indians, and, in August of 1757, he moved against Fort William Henry by bateaux and canoes. He besieged the fort for six days before the British surrendered, after receiving the promise that Montcalm would escort them with "their arms and other honors of war" to Fort Edward. However, Montcalm's Indians had no stomach for European military niceties. They made the British run the gantlet before a shocked Montcalm, who managed to halt the massacre by supposedly baring his breast and shouting to the Indians, "Kill me but spare the English, who are under my protection." This noble plea had some effect on the red men, but not before thirty Englishmen were killed and Fort William Henry was completely destroyed. If his soldiers hadn't been needed in Quebec to bring in the harvest and prevent a famine, Montcalm could have chased the British right back to Albany. He returned home, leaving the British confused and humiliated.

The famine came anyway, through crop failure and an

efficient British naval blockade. Montcalm's victorious army shrank in spirit and number throughout the following year. England could have taken advantage of this, but, in the words of a distinguished North Country historian, Winslow C. Watson, "Britain sent to her colonies effete generals, bankrupt nobles and debauched parasites of the court. France selected her functionaries from the wisest, noblest and best of her people, and, therefore, her colonial interests were usually directed with wisdom and sagacity." Finally, in the winter of 1758, the British tried to feel out the French. They sent Rogers and 180 of his Rangers to reconnoiter Fort Carillon. Rogers was ambushed by some French Indians, who carried back to Montcalm 140 Ranger scalps. (Rogers himself escaped by his celebrated "slide" off a huge rock into Lake George; actually, he turned his snowshoes around and followed another trail behind the rock down to the lake's shore, leading the Indians to believe that he had walked toward the rock and miraculously leapt or slid off it to freedom. Rogers' Rock still attracts a bemused crowd during the summer tourist season.)

All else having failed, the British raised a massive force of seven thousand regulars (including the famous Black Watch Regiment) and nine thousand provincials, and, with a stupendous array of artillery, sent this splendid army down Lake George in more than a thousand bateaux, whale boats, and rafts. It was by all accounts the grandest sight yet seen in North America. Its crucial drawback was that the entire force was put under the

command of another hopeless fop and blunderer, General James Abercromby. The general, positive that he couldn't lose against a dispirited enemy one quarter his size, set up headquarters well behind the lines and attacked before his artillery arrived. The infantry beat the French in a forest near Fort Carillon, but, repeating the mistake of three years before, the British didn't push on to the fort, choosing instead to bivouac nearby. This gave Montcalm plenty of time to erect gigantic breastworks out of spruce and pine between the fort and the British. The next morning, Abercromby ordered wave after wave of luckless soldiers against the well-protected French. Each wave was thrown back with horrifying losses (the Black Watch Regiment alone lost over half its men, which later moved Robert Louis Stevenson to write the ballad, "Ticonderoga"). At last, Abercromby ordered retreat, characteristically leading the way back to Lake George himself. Retreat quickly turned into rout and rout into panic. The French, amazingly, lost only five hundred men; the British lost thousands.

For the third time in a decade, the English had to take stock of themselves as far as control of Lake Champlain—and thus the North American continent—was concerned. William Pitt was instrumental in having Abercromby recalled to England and replaced by the infinitely more capable General Jeffrey Amherst. Meanwhile, continued famine was depopulating Canada and Montcalm saw disaster approaching. He wrote a friend in France: "There are situations where nothing remains for a general but to

die with honor." He withdrew most of his forces from Lake Champlain to defend Quebec against an expected attack by General James Wolfe, leaving General Boulamarque and twenty-three hundred men behind. It wasn't nearly enough. In July of 1759, Amherst gathered a large army and, once again, a splendid fleet sailed down Lake George to take Fort Carillon. Boulamarque decided on a scorched-earth policy. He blew up Fort Carillon, Fort St. Frédéric, and the settlements around them, and retreated to the north. Lake Champlain was handed over to Amherst almost without bloodshed, which so excited the general that he ordered Fort Carillon reconstructed and renamed Ticonderoga (from the Indian "Tia-on-ta-roken," or "Point between two lakes"). And once he saw the potential of Crown Point, he ordered an entirely new structure built there called, less imaginatively, Fort Crown Point. It was three times the size of Ticonderoga and cost more than ten million dollars, and was at the time the most ambitious and expensive fortification anywhere in North America. Fort Crown Point was never fully completed because in September Wolfe defeated Montcalm at the Battle of Quebec, New France fell to England, and, after years of hot, bloody importance, the Lake Champlain forts were suddenly redundant.

With the French banished forever from the Champlain Valley by virtue of the Treaty of Paris, Louis XV's generous land grants to his soldiers were repudiated by the British king, who proceeded to authorize new patents to *his* soldiers. The English grants ranged down through the

ranks from five thousand acres to a field officer to fifty for a private, with "all mines of gold and silver, and all pine trees fit for masts" reserved for the crown. The first zoning law in the territory of what was to become Essex County was also stipulated: Not more than one family per one thousand acres and at least three of every fifty arable acres had to be cultivated within three years. As for the vast Iroquois lands inland from the lake, the crown merely declared that they were under the sovereignty and "protection" of the king, and that was that. Indians could sell land to the white men, but the titles had to pass to the crown first, with attendant service fees. (The Indians never really recognized this royal declaration, but the approaching revolution made the argument academic anyway.)

Several discharged British soldiers, perhaps entranced by the scenery more than anything else, took advantage of the king's offer. A few of them actually stuck it out through the first winter, but most sold quickly and cheaply to the first comer. The first comer was usually a shrewd Boston or New York City land speculator who knew a good thing when he saw (or rather heard about) it. The first of several North Country land grabs was on.

A new farming and trading settlement was growing on the site of the old French village around Fort Crown Point. Services were established, including a blacksmith's shop run by a scoundrel named Gilfoil who prospered by selling crowbars stolen from the fort as fine steel harrow teeth. He also stamped out brass discs from officers' trunk

straps, and these "Gilfoil's coppers" became the Crown Point currency at fourteen to the shilling. But it was another enterprising Irishman, William Gilliland, who really started things moving in Essex County.

Born in Caddy, Ireland, in 1734, Gilliland received a fair education despite his low birth. As a young man, he made the critical mistake of falling in love with an aristocratic heiress, and he was promptly compelled to leave Ireland via the British Army. He was sent to the Colonies —it is speculated that he may even have fought at Ticonderoga—and, after his discharge, he settled in New York City, where he worked for a wealthy merchant named Phagan. Phagan had a daughter, Elizabeth, and Gilliland, true to form, lost little time in winning her and her attractive dowry of fifteen hundred pounds. Seeing himself as the holder of grand estates, like the ones he had been so rudely denied in Ireland, he bought for one hundred pounds about two thousand acres of land north of Crown Point. Other land became available from ex-soldiers anxious to sell, and soon he owned over twenty thousand acres along Lake Champlain around the mouth of the Boquet River. He hired mechanics and laborers in New York City, provided them with tools and supplies, and, with their respective wives, a minister, his own family, and a "negro man" he whimsically dubbed Ireland, he set off for the wilderness on May 10, 1765, to settle his unseen estates. At Albany they picked up two drovers and twenty oxen, twenty cows, one bull, and some calves, and this strange assemblage embarked in four bateaux up

the Hudson for Fort Edward. Articulate and thorough, Gilliland kept a careful journal of his early adventures, detailing the arduous trip, the wonders and hardships of the North Country, and the problems of controlling his people in "the howling wilderness," as he called it.

On June 1, they arrived at Ticonderoga and spent days portaging the bateaux and cattle over the short strip of land between Lake George and Lake Champlain. Finally, they made it to his properties at the mouth of the Boquet, which he immediately named Willsboro, in honor of himself. (Elizabethtown was later named for his wife, whose dowry, after all, had launched the project; Bessboro, now called Westport, was named for a daughter.) At Willsboro, they found fertile land, ideal streams for sawmills, and excellent fishing ("Having thrown out our fishing seine we hauled in sixty large fish, being mostly maskinonge, bass and pickerel," he wrote in his journal.) The Gilliland pioneers set right to work. They cleared land, built roads, made maple syrup, planted wheat, slaughtered cattle, explored and surveyed, nursed and sometimes buried each other, fought the winter, and managed to attract even more settlers, to whom Gilliland lent money and leased lots for tidy sums. Many settlers could not take the rigors of North Country life or Gilliland's highhandedness (he appointed himself the sole judge and jury in all disputes). Several fled, only to be caught or return on their own for their wives. Gilliland even had a servant problem: "Robert McLane and George Wilson," he wrote, "quit my employ the 2nd June 1766 and went

off, the former having enticed away my bound servant maid Mary Craig—she being great with child to him."

He held his debtors in a kind of slavery and he wasn't afraid to use force to back up his authority, often calling on the small British garrisons at Ticonderoga and Crown Point to help him out. He was finally commissioned a justice of the peace, which lent an official flavor to his judgments. But then, in March of 1775, a remarkable thing happened; the people of Willsboro banded together and drafted a humble covenant, the preamble of which read:

> We the subscribers, inhabitants of Willsboro, finding it necessary to make regulations concerning roads, fences, bridges, and hogs, have this day assembled for that purpose, and have entered into the following resolves. To be binding on us respectively, by every tie of honor and honesty, for the space of twelve months from this date, and also to be equally binding on such other persons as may become inhabitants of this settlement during the said term, which resolves are entered upon by a majority of votes.

Democratic government had somehow burst upon this speck of civilization in the wilderness a full year before the Declaration of Independence was drafted. It had the effect of a diminutive, grass-roots American Revolution. And, of equal significance, the Willsboro townspeople had persuaded Gilliland to sign the extraordinary document. Perhaps Gilliland agreed in order to keep the peace

in his restless colony; about that time he had dreamed up a much more grandiose scheme than merely making his fortune on the west shore of Lake Champlain. There was at the south end of the lake a counterpart to the enterprising Irishman named Philip Skene, who, like Gilliland, had formed a self-serving pioneer colony called Skenesboro (now Whitehall, New York). The two moguls found inspiration in each other's company and together they conspired to merge their power and people. The result of such a merger was to be a separate province, with its capital at Crown Point and its political structure ruled by Skene and Gilliland. This private nation, as it were, would extend from the St. Lawrence River on the west to the Connecticut River on the east, and from Canada on the north to as far south as they dared to go. Considering the influence in the area of the two men, it just might have worked—except that war came to Essex County again.

The British military influence along Lake Champlain had faded to practically nothing. The once monumental forts were allowed to deteriorate, discipline was lax, and a fire in the powder magazine of Fort Crown Point ruined the most expensive symbol of English might in the New World. While plans were made for rebuilding the fort, the heavy guns were moved south to Ticonderoga. This maneuver caught the eye of a boorish but highly literate outlaw from across the lake, Ethan Allen, who was in serious trouble with the New York colonial powers for opposing their claim to much of what is now Vermont.

When he heard about the battle with the British at Lexington and Concord, in April of 1775, he immediately assembled his rowdy Green Mountain Boys. He had nothing to lose; there was a British reward of a hundred and fifty pounds on his head anyway. He set his sights on Ticonderoga and the heavy artillery there. But so had Benedict Arnold, a deserter from the British Colonial Militia who had arrived at Allen's headquarters with a commission from the Massachusetts Safety Committee and a small band of patriots. Allen and Arnold were soon at each other's throats over who was going to command the expedition. Allen, on home ground, won the argument and, permitting Arnold to accompany him, led eighty-three of his men across the lake to Ticonderoga. A spy was sent into the fort, posing as a man in desperate need of a barber. The spy received a passable haircut and later reported to Allen that the fort and its complement of forty-nine Redcoats, forty-five sheep, eleven cows, two children, and one wife were in poor shape. Heady with this intelligence, Allen brazenly filed up to the sally port of Ticonderoga before dawn of May 10, 1775. The sleepy sentinel snapped his musket, which misfired, and he ran for his life to the barracks within, closely followed by Allen and company. The garrison awakened and came out on the parade ground to see what was going on. A Captain Delaplace appeared in his nightgown and was told by Allen to surrender. By what authority? asked the blear-eyed captain, to which Allen responded with those immortal words: "By the authority of the Great Jehovah

and the Continental Congress!" Captain Delaplace had certainly heard of the Great Jehovah but he probably was ignorant of the Continental Congress. Allen's drawn sword over his head gave him some notion, however, and the garrison, more than one hundred cannon, and ninety gallons of rum were taken into captivity. For the rest of the day, according to Allen's account, the victors of the first aggressive action of the American Revolution "tossed about the flowing bowl and wished success to Congress and the liberty and freedom of America."

Probably hung over but game, Allen and his boys took Fort Crown Point the following day (manned by only a sergeant and ten Redcoats), while another band of his men captured Skenesboro, with its Tory leader, Philip Skene, and his schooner. (Recommissioned as the *Liberty*, the schooner was the first American naval vessel.) The news of these easy triumphs over the British made the rebels dizzy with excitement. However, the Continental Congress, whose name Allen had so proudly invoked, was something less than pleased. Congress was terrified of England's reaction. Allen was ordered to remove Ticonderoga's cannon to the head of Lake George, so that "they may be safely returned when the restoration of harmony between Great Britain and her colonies, so ardently desired by the latter, shall render it prudent and consistent with the over-ruling law of self-preservation." Allen flatly refused, and it was fortunate he did. A few months later, his brute arrogance was justified when the artillery was hauled through the wilderness from Ticonderoga to

Boston, where it saved the day for General Washington.

With most of the British troops tied up in Boston and with French-Canadian sentiment on the side of the Americans, it seemed to Arnold and Allen an ideal time to invade Canada. Throughout the following year, they tried, overland and by Lake Champlain, but they lost out miserably to the British regulars, the loyal Iroquois (who quite correctly feared the cocky Americans), the North Country winter, and smallpox. The tattered, sick survivors retreated to Fort Crown Point, later abandoning it to make their stand at the more sturdy Ticonderoga.

Arnold appointed himself commander of the American fleet, which was being built at Skenesboro, from native pine and spruce, and fitted out at Ticonderoga. General Guy Carleton, in the fall of 1776, brought his British fleet south to meet Arnold, and the first important naval battle of the Revolution took place off Valcour Island, just north of Essex County. (The remains of this battle are still being brought up from the lake's bottom by skindivers.) Carleton and his more experienced sailors won easily enough, but—like so many British commanders before him—he didn't make the most of it. He retired to Canada for the winter, giving the Americans time to strengthen Ticonderoga.

Gilliland, meanwhile, had shrewdly sided with the patriots, unlike his friend and fellow conspirator, Philip Skene. In a memorial written by Gilliland in 1777, he took credit for all sorts of patriotic acts, among them the original plan to seize Ticonderoga and Crown Point from

the British, keeping the peace between Allen and Arnold, the formal induction into the American forces of the Green Mountain Boys, and the raising of a company of minutemen from his Boquet colonists. Indeed, the British posted an attractive reward for Gilliland's arrest, and some of his more disgruntled tenants tried to collect it, with the help of a sheriff, four Tories, and three Indians. Gilliland captured the lot of them and had them imprisoned at Crown Point. For all his troubles, Gilliland had the incredible distinction of being accused of disloyalty by none other than Benedict Arnold. Arnold filed formal charges against him with General Gates stating that Gilliland had bilked Arnold's troops after their retreat from Canada to Crown Point and had called them "a parcel of damned robbers." Gilliland may well have used such language, or worse, because Arnold had urged his soldiers to ravage the colony's crops and property, even after Gilliland had extended his hospitality to the sick and bedraggled men. The erstwhile Baron of Essex County was later cleared of Arnold's charges, but the damage had already been done. The colony on the Boquet River was a shambles and the settlers were running for their lives.

Arnold's plundering of his own countrymen had been bad enough, but in the spring of 1777 General John Burgoyne and a crack force of English regulars, Canadians, German mercenaries, and Indians sailed up Lake Champlain to recapture Ticonderoga and cut off New England from the Middle-Atlantic States. They encamped near what was left of Willsboro, where Burgoyne made an im-

passioned speech to the Indians that served to fan their already hot hatred of the American colonists. After the speech not a single Willsboro building was left standing, and every breathing revolutionist made his way to Ticonderoga for the last-ditch stand. Nevertheless, Burgoyne quickly took the fort by the simple expedient of hauling his cannon up supposedly inaccessible Mount Defiance, overlooking the hapless bastion, and pouring fire onto the heads of the Americans. A nighttime evacuation was bungled and patriots scattered to the south in panic, with the British and their allies close behind.

The fall of Ticonderoga set all England cheering and all that was left of America bickering. But the Americans managed to collect themselves enough to check Burgoyne north of Albany. Then, the rough Adirondack woods, lack of supplies, Indian defections, and guerrilla warfare harassed Burgoyne even more. While waiting for reinforcements at Saratoga, he was attacked and sharply defeated. He surrendered on October 17th. A band of rebels, keeping together in the night by hooting like owls, later struck Ticonderoga; they freed more than one hundred prisoners, but the fort itself wouldn't fall. It was finally abandoned by the remaining British troops when news of Burgoyne's surrender reached them, and Fort Ticonderoga never again saw serious military action. Throughout the rest of the revolution, raiding parties occasionally camped there, but British ships of the line became the real guardians of Lake Champlain until hostilities ended at Yorktown. General Washington made a victorious

inspection of both Crown Point and Ticonderoga in 1783, but what he saw was mostly sad ruins. Crown Point quickly reverted to pastureland and Ticonderoga was disposed of in a grant to Columbia and Union Colleges by the new State of New York.

TODAY, the Crown Point peninsula is a serene, pastoral place. It seems to be dozing in another century, except for two modern phenomena—the sleek Lake Champlain Bridge, connecting Vermont and New York, and Roland W. Robbins. Robbins is a compact, intense archeologist who bears the face and accent of an unreconstructed New England Yankee. Since June of 1968, he has commuted once a week, in a car with the indicative license plate HIDDEN, from his home in Lincoln, Massachusetts, to Crown Point in order to supervise digs at various likely spots on the peninsula. A specialist in colonial and early American landmark preservation, Robbins has already successfully unearthed and explored Thoreau's Walden Pond cabin site, the Sleepy

Hollow Dutch trading post at Tarrytown, and John Alden's home in Duxbury, Massachusetts. Yet, he avoids such titles as historian or archeologist. "I'm a pick-and-shovel man, an excavator, really," he told a friend who accompanied him on a tour of his Crown Point digs. "And here, it's a pick-and-shovel man's dream come true. There probably isn't any more outstanding colonial military and historical find than Crown Point."

Robbins explained that it wasn't until the beginning of the twentieth century that New York State fully realized what a treasure Crown Point was, when it acquired the ruins of the forts there from individuals who had used the land for private purposes. Slowly, the state has been buying up more land around the ruins, until now only one private house exists at the very tip of the point. (Only recently did the federal government get around to designating Crown Point as a National Park Service Historical Landmark.) The New York State Historical Trust and the Crown Point Foundation—the latter, a nonprofit institution whose distinguished trustees include Robbins himself—hired a crew of professional earth movers, enlisted some student volunteers, put them all at Robbins's disposal, and told them to go to work.

"Years ago, the state sponsored a rough restoration of Amherst's Fort Crown Point," Robbins said, "and that plus our little museum, a bathing beach, and a picnic area are run by the Conservation Department people. The fort attracts some tourists in the summer, but they run all over the place writing their names on the walls

and dropping beer cans and candy wrappers. A few come to see Rodin's bust, *La Belle France,* in the Champlain Memorial Lighthouse near the bridge, but most days, it's hardly worth opening the gates. The work I'm doing isn't just for whatever tourists show up. You see, the fact that the French left their gracious Fort St. Frédéric in such a blithering hurry, blowing it sky high in 1759 so the English couldn't use it, was an enormous break for us." Robbins pointed to a deep trench being widened by a worker surgically operating a power shovel. "This was once the moat of Fort St. Frédéric," he went on. "Notice the retaining walls there. When the British arrived, the moat was the natural place to dump things, to clean up the mess—and there was plenty of mess around to bury. The British and two centuries of earth covered it up very nicely. Once I figured out where the moat was and started to dig, I found piles of stuff—everything from rum bottles to broken bayonets and moose bones—all in a beautifully preserved state, just as if they were left by some picnickers a few days ago. A lot of this stuff is still junk, but most of it is remarkable evidence of how soldiers and settlers lived at the time, both the British and French. And you come across a bit of historical gossip, too. For instance, the other day we dug up a very old cannon near the moat. Now that in itself wasn't so surprising—although it's a lovely old gun—but what interested me was that the cannon predated the French cannon of the time by a couple of hundred years. This leads me to suspect that Louis XV tried to dump his old hard-

ware on the colonists, keeping the better, more modern stuff for France proper. That explains a lot militarily; a good cannon could make a decisive difference in a battle. Later on, the French were probably kicking themselves for being so stingy."

Robbins walked lovingly through the excavation of the Light Infantry Redoubt, a valuable find uncovered behind Fort St. Frédéric in the early months of his digging. "Look at these walls and passageways," he said. "Look how beautifully they built things then!" He caressed a chunk of limestone which fitted squarely into the jigsaw puzzle of the bastion. "What I'm really trying to do here is preserve these wonderful ruins, not rebuild them. I want them to be exposed but still be ruins, so people can use their own historical imagination. Restoration can sometimes look pretty cheap, like an amusement park. Like that Frontier Land, down the road there in North Hudson. I want to find the basic pattern of all the historical sites just underfoot. It's so close to us and yet so elusive. Hidden, always hidden. But I usually find more than I expect. I've already got enough artifacts and relics to fill a new museum. And there's still so much to do—the old lime kilns, another redoubt, the rest of Amherst's great fortifications, and God knows what else is beneath what we're walking on. I don't think I can live long enough to finish Crown Point."

Fort Ticonderoga, on the other hand, has been restored to within an inch of its several lives. In 1816, a New York merchant, William Ferris Pell, leased the grounds around

the fort from Columbia and Union Colleges, and four years later he bought the land and the fort ruins outright. He built a handsome hotel called the Pavilion on the lake just east of the fort, and this became the first tourist attraction in Essex County, at a time when interest in the nation's short history was just awakening. The rich made the Pavilion a must stop on the popular "Northern Grand Tour" of the 1800's. Part of the charm of the place was the presence of Archibald Pell, who managed the Pavilion and was in the habit of saluting every passing lake steamer with a blast from a small cannon he kept handy. One day, however, he—or perhaps a sleepless neighbor or guest—overloaded the cannon before a steamer went by, and Mr. Pell was instantly dispatched to a greater reward. Despite this tragedy, the Pell family maintained a deep concern for Ticonderoga. Stephen Pell, in 1908, began the restoration of the fort and the stocking of its military museum. It was opened to the public the following year, with the formal ceremonies attended by President Taft. Ever since then the Pells have continued the restoration until now only the East Barracks want rebuilding. They established the nonprofit Fort Ticonderoga Association to run the fort, museum, gift shop, and restaurant, and it all operates very efficiently.

But it is restored too well. With flags of all the powers that ever had anything to do with the site flapping in the lake breeze over the barracks and demilunes, the fort gives the uneasy impression of having been built a few weeks ago as a set of some Charlton Heston movie. "Inac-

cessible" Mount Defiance still lurks ominously over the fort and the view from the walls is quite striking, but with tourists peering at everything through cameras and their children brandishing souvenir tomahawks, the place is contemporized even more. There is almost no room for what Roland Robbins calls the "historical imagination."

Immediately after the revolution, the devastated lands on the west shore of Lake Champlain were inhabited by only an occasional trapper, a few unhappy soldiers, and the wolves. Most of the Indians, who had used the wilderness as their own preserve for centuries, fled to Canada out of justified fear of American vengeance. The old hunting grounds became the property of the State of New York, with a handful of Indian reservations provided for in treaties, most of which are hardly honored today. As time passed, some of Gilliland's surviving original colonists began to trickle back to rebuild their holdings near the Boquet, but Gilliland himself was in and out of jail on a variety of charges, including Arnold's accusation of treason, indebtedness, fraudulent practices in land sales, and illegal recovery of deserted slaves. He had lost not only most of his slaves, his power, and his property (worth an estimated seventy thousand pounds) but also his mind. After a six-year stretch in a New York City prison—during which time he wrote several touching but ineffective petitions—he was finally freed and allowed to return to the land of his former triumphs. He lived with relatives in the renascent village of Essex and took to

roaming madly about the countryside as if he still owned it. In the winter of 1796, he set out across ice-covered Lake Champlain to visit his friend and early surveyor of the region, Platt Rogers, in Vermont. The old entrepreneur was found frozen to death in the hills near the lake, his hands and knees worn raw from crawling about aimlessly. He is buried in a cemetery at Essex, and Gilliland's descendants still come to visit the grave site, a simple shrine to the pioneer life.

Had Gilliland not run afoul of the new American laws and kept his sanity, he would have seen most of his hopes fulfilled. By 1783, a surge of immigration hit Essex County. It was called "New York Fever." The virus was spread throughout New England by Revolutionary War veterans who had seen tall stands of virgin timber, fertile land along the lake, and an abundance of fish and game all going begging. The Adirondack country was the wild, wide-open West of the day. Opportunity was there, it seemed, and hundreds of exhilarated New Englanders, especially Vermonters, crossed the lake by sled or boat with their families and oxen and a few necessary tools.

It was a pioneer story that was to repeat itself for another century all over America. Instant settlements sprouted through community action. Every person strong enough to hold an axe pitched in to clear the land and help erect a rough but livable log cabin for each newly arrived neighbor, often in just one day's time. Logging bees were held to level the fields for corn and wheat planting. Some stock was raised, but venison was always

plentiful. Few pieces of furniture from a more gracious life were hauled into the wilderness, so the pioneers improvised beds, tables, and chairs out of the seemingly endless supply of hard- and softwoods around. The novel spirit of American democracy was infectious, as people worked together to construct roads, schools, churches, water-powered sawmills, crude flour-grinding devices out of hollowed stumps and sapling-hung rocks, and even iron forges, which put to good use the ore that was literally bursting from the ground. A blockhouse was built in Essex as protection against an expected Indian uprising that never took place; it was easily converted into a courthouse and jail, and the first semblance of organized government in the wilderness since the 1775 Willsboro convenant appeared. The village of Essex became the county's first seat and even lent its good name.

But the communal advantages of pioneer life were more than outweighed by the hardships, both natural and man-made. As soon as the immigration tide looked serious, the state government decided to sell titles to the wilderness real estate the immigrants thought was free. Many settlers discovered, after they had laboriously cleared and sown their land, that it really belonged to some speculator from the city, who inevitably turned up with deed in hand insisting on his rent or the land itself. This led to quarrels and quarrels led to shooting and blood flowed again in the North Country. But the law was on the landowners' side. Soon, one way or another, the arable lowlands near the lake were all accounted for.

New pioneers had to push west to the mountains, where they found the stony hillsides no better, and often worse, for farming than the hillsides of New England. The less tenacious among them grew thoroughly disgusted and moved even farther west, to the St. Lawrence plains and the land along Lake Ontario and Lake Erie.

As for the natural hardships, the written testimony of a Mrs. Adolphus Sheldon, who emigrated to Ticonderoga in 1797, is a graphic example:

> "We came through from the head of Lake George on an awful cold day on the ice. . . . There both sides and the whole length of lake the great pines stood all around on the mountains, one unbroken wilderness. . . . We had heard that Ti was a paradise, that we should find pigs and fowls ready cooked running about with knives and forks stuck in their backs, crying 'Eat us!' But when we got there it was all bushes. . . . On the 15th of April came snow breast deep and there we were. It was a terrible storm—you could walk over the fences, and we gathered sap on snow shoes. We all went cutting logs and when we got four walls locked together, half a roof and the chamber floor, we moved in. When we wanted groceries we had to cross the lake to J. Catlin's for them, but oftener went without them. We had brown bread, and wheat cracked in milk. Land alive! when we wanted fish, all we had to do was to run down to the brook—there were schools of them

big as a washtub. Father drew out eighteen great trout one morning, I remember, in about three minutes. . . . No sheep. Land! You could have no sheep; the wolves would tear you right down. You could hear them away off in the night—one would howl, then another would answer—howl, howl—then another, way off, howl, howl, howl,—till they got up such a roar that it would almost tear you down. One day I and my brother were standing on the bridge and three wolves came along the road close to us. We thought they were three gray dogs till they got near, and then we scampered, I tell you. Oh! They were awful thick and dangerous. We never had any sheep. You could not keep any. The animals we feared most were bears, wolves, catamounts and rattlesnakes. . . . Gracious! we didn't have any calico. Calico was worth a dollar a yard! . . . Father made his own shoes. I made my own with cloth and old felt hat for soles. Went barefoot in summer. . . . After we were married we moved across the valley westward to the Sheldon place where we had to tough it. I had toughed it at father's and now I had to tough it here. Only half an acre was cleared. There we lived five years without a stove or fireplace. We absolutely had no chimney. We burned wood right against the logs of the cabin and when they got afire we put it out. Sap from the maple trees was so plenty that we could hear it in the night, drip, drip, drip, till morning. Deer used to come and stand

right across the run where I used to get water, and once one knocked down the door of my oven not two rods from the house, but he didn't get the pie crust. . . . Now came a trouble upon us. My husband had just got a grand fallow burned as black as coal, had worked out and paid for seed wheat, been to get it, and coming home in getting over a log fell and almost cut his hand in two on his sickle. He came home after I was abed, groaning: 'I've cut me to death.' . . . I halloed and yelled to make distant neighbors hear and could hear nothing but George Cook's sheep bleat and the patter of rain on the leaves. It rained dreadfully that night. At last a woman that lived on the mountain above us came, but she could do nothing. I resolved to make a desperate attempt, for we believed that my husband would die. So I seized a great firebrand and ran. I had no shoes or stockings but I swung my firebrand ahead and each side to scare the wolves as I ran along the edge of the mountain and crossed the valley to my father's place. Only a few days before my husband had come along the path with a leg of mutton. He set it down on the leaves a minute and the next day around that place half an acre of leaves was torn by the wolves. When I had crossed the brook I heard something splash in the water behind me. The rain roared so I could not hear for sure but I thought it might be something and looked back but could see nothing. I tell you the grass did not grow under my

feet that trip. It was not bears or rattlesnakes this time but wolves, wolves! . . . I heard Mrs. Wardwell from my house, crying out, murder! murder! I cried back and my folks thought it was to them, and so they cried to me and the doctor a little beyond with my brother to them. I to her, they to me, and my brother and the doctor to them, and so it kept up a stream of halloes and yells through the woods. It was a wild time but I only thought of my husband. He was three weeks getting well. I did every thing. . . . I must tell you about one or two tussles we had with bears. There was one that come into our cornfield and used to tear it down like a dozen hogs. My husband tried every way, and at last set a gun for her just before dark. 'Now old woman,' said he, 'when that gun goes off you must go with me and I will find the bear.' Just as we were getting into bed bang went the old gun. 'Here we are,' said I. He seized a big brand and I followed him out into the clearing. 'Give me the brand,' said I. 'Just as well,' said he, 'I'll go forward and find the old critter.' 'Take care,' I warned him, 'if she is wounded, old man, she will make shoe strings of your hide.' No, he would not hear to the old woman. He had not gone far when he tumbled right over the bear. He hopped up, I guess near two feet at the bear's growl, and cried, a short quick cry, 'O God!' Bear weighed 200 pounds, we tried the fat; the meat cut like pork, but I could not bear to eat it. . . . When I had nothing to do I

helped my husband. I did not care what I wore, had or did—anything to help him. I worked there and was black as a nigger. We lived, as you might say, on work and love."

Among these privations was that old bugaboo—money. There was little in the way of crop surplus, so few settlers carried their produce to distant markets. Yet, when the county lines became official and townships formed and the population grew, money had to be found somewhere to pay taxes, equip schools, and buy better tools for land clearing. Bartering was the common currency until Yankee ingenuity came up with a satchel of fiscal tricks. With wood as abundant as fresh water, almost every family was living in the midst of the raw materials for the simple home industry of potash making. One merely burned timber, leached the ashes, and then boiled out the lye, which was eagerly bought up by itinerant merchants for soap and explosives. The merchants paid half in cash and half in goods. Other enterprising folk set up distilleries, when it was discovered that rye could be cultivated more easily than wheat and that rum could be manufactured from maple syrup. At the going price of only twenty cents a gallon, liquor was as available as birch beer and drunk as copiously. This particular home industry lasted in Essex County right down through Prohibition, and some say it's still thriving in a few backwoods quarters. The demand has never slackened.

If settlers claimed that mountain dew was essential for

snake bites, they were more than likely telling the truth. Snakes, particularly rattlesnakes, abounded in the pioneer days and they were the source of yet another moneymaking scheme. Snake oil was an accepted cure for rheumatism and other ills, and rattlesnake hunters could also make a few dollars by selling the skins or by exhibiting the live exotic creatures in Albany to terrified city folk. One Elisha Belden of Ticonderoga was famous throughout the county as a hunter with a magical power over rattlers. Armed with only a crotched stick, he would enter a notorious cavern called Rattlesnake Den and mysteriously charm the inhabitants into a basket. His last trip to the den was made on a Sunday, when Mr. Belden neglected to change from his church clothes. He was found some hours later quite swollen, blackened, and dead. A local chronicler of the event explained that "it was because the varmints did not know him, as he was dressed up and had on white stockings—they thought he was Judge Kellog." It should be added that a half-empty whisky bottle was discovered next to the corpse.

Panthers, wolves, and other predators had to be exterminated if the settlements were to prosper, and this, too, brought in cash for North Country men through generous bounties. At an 1806 town meeting in Elizabethtown, it was voted to declare an award of three dollars for every wolf killed in the county, a rather large sum for the day. The better shots among the settlers turned up their noses at tedious farming duties and made for the woods with rifle in hand to have some fun and, in passing, earn their

living. The result was that a wolf or panther hasn't been seen in the area for fifty years. (A law still on the state books says that wolf heads turned in for bounties must have the ears removed and burned. This statute came about because wily hunters would pass around the same old wolf's head, collecting on it each time from the county clerk. The law also states, of course, that no bounties will be paid on earless wolves.)

Some men made an excellent living from fur trapping, trading their pelts with Vermonters across Lake Champlain. Crude ferries handled the growing traffic at first, but, in the early 1800's, the second steamboat in the world, the *Vermont*, was built by an associate of Robert Fulton and put into operation on the lake. The North Country was beginning to live up to its promise.

As new settlers were pushed inland to the poor, heavily forested soil of the mountains, as others were driven off their property by patent disputes, and as the long, discouraging winters made agriculture less endearing, the real value of timber cutting became apparent. Virgin spruce, pine, hemlock, and various hardwoods were everywhere; the problem was to find a way to get them to market. The obvious market was Quebec and the easiest way to get wood there was to float the logs down rivers to Lake Champlain, then lash the logs into massive lumber rafts for the journey north. The lake was soon clogged with rafts propelled by sail and oar, heading on the five-day adventure to the Richelieu River and Quebec. By 1812, the timber trade was all the thing, some modest for-

tunes were being made, eight county towns were chartered with a total population of ten thousand, and then, incredibly, war came again.

The War of 1812 didn't actually arrive in Essex County till the summer of 1813. The people knew or cared very little about the reasons for the conflict—impressed seamen and Napoleon meant next to nothing to pioneers with their own serious troubles—but they did sense that the British in Canada, good timber customers though they were, might want to add flourishing northern New York to the empire. And that was exactly the case. In July of 1813, a small British fleet sailed up the Boquet River and landed a party bent on seizing flour stored near Willsboro. The soldiers destroyed whatever property they encountered, until a hastily assembled militia led by an impromptu general beat them back. The British, minus a galley and several troops, retreated to Canada.

That incident infuriated the people of Essex to a high war pitch. The lucrative Quebec timber market was forgotten. Rumors of a large-scale invasion spread to every backwoods cabin, and it was clear that the people would have to defend their own land. Men gathered up anything that could serve as a weapon, women packed salt pork and johnnycake into knapsacks, village greens were turned into training grounds, and by the spring of 1814 a sizable, if motley, militia was ready. The British strategy was the same as in the revolution—to split the eastern states from the rest of America along the axis of Lake Champlain and the Hudson. This time, about fifteen

thousand troops, many of them tough veterans from Wellington's campaigns, marched towards Plattsburgh, a Champlain port just north of Essex County. An American force of about four thousand regulars and militiamen moved to the Saranac River to meet the invasion, while a comparably outnumbered naval squadron, commanded by Captain Thomas MacDonough, sailed north to engage the British fleet. As delighted but dispassionate spectators watched from the Vermont shore (New Englanders, by and large, managed to resist the war fever), the two armadas clashed and the British got the worse of it. The land forces were skirmishing along the Saranac when news of MacDonough's victory reached the troops. They gave three cheers, which the British took to mean victory on land, as well. The Redcoats once again retreated to Canada, leaving two thousand dead behind; the Americans lost less than one hundred and fifty. North Country patriots were justifiably full of themselves. They had helped to defeat a great world power twice within forty years. A derisive ditty about the British, popular among the Essex settlers, summed up the spirit of the postwar era:

> Now the battle's growing hot, boys, I don't know
>   how 'twill turn
> While MacDonough's boats, on swivels hung, contin-
>   ually do burn:
> We see such constant flashing that the smoke be-
>   clouds the day,

And our larger boats have struck and the small ones run away.
We've got too far from Canada, run for life, boys, run.

One of the stalwarts who had sent the British running for their lives was a local legend named Joseph Call, better known as "The Lewis Giant." Although he was only six feet tall and weighed less than two hundred pounds, Call could perform astounding feats of strength and was unbeatable as a wrestler. (It was said of him, by way of explanation, that he was double-jointed, that his ribs had grown together, and that he had two sets of teeth.) A millwright and lumberjack, Joe Call joined the militia during the 1814 hostilities and won wide fame by such tricks as lifting one-ton cannon and dispensing cider to thirsty troops from a huge barrel carried on his shoulder as easily as a musket. And when he locked his arms and legs around a tree, a team of oxen couldn't tear him loose.

Both his curse and his glory was that every man who fancied himself a wrestler wanted to challenge him. Sometimes the results were laughable; Call would allow the challenger to attempt intricate holds and then, tiring of the joke, he would slowly raise the unlucky fellow into the air and dance about with him at arm's length, shouting, "Now let's rassle!" One other time, however, a British grenadier appeared in Plattsburgh after the war and boasted that he could throw any goddam Yankee, even the great Joe Call. That sort of talk from an arrogant re-

cent enemy amused the Lewis Giant, who effortlessly pinned the man. The humiliated grenadier tried to kill Call and ended up crushed to death by the enraged titan's bare hands. His fame continued to spread and he was challenged by fighters from abroad. A favorite Essex County story concerns a professional English wrestler who arrived in the village of Lewis to arrange a match with Call, who was plowing a field at the time. The Englishman, not recognizing his opponent, asked the plowman where he might find the famous Lewis Giant. Joe Call picked up his plow with one hand and calmly pointed with it at a nearby farmhouse. The challenger was out of the county within the hour. Billed as "Modern Hercules," Call went on tour all over the world, winning prizes and honors. He returned to his home in Lewis in 1834 and promptly died from, of all things, a carbuncle on his neck. He is still talked about by some as if he died yesterday.

For the first time, really, the people of Essex County considered their land safely their own. It had been fought for, worked over, disputed by speculators, fought for again, and, at last, made truly productive. After the war, every citizen set himself to the, even then, good old American task of making as much money as possible. Timber was again the way to the quick killing, either by cutting it into lumber, burning it for potash or forge-firing charcoal, or stripping hemlock bark to use as a tanning material.

A second surge of immigration hit the county. French-Canadians came south to work as lumberjacks, and a cry went out for even more raw muscle power to drive teams, build roads, operate sawmills, run logs, and oar lumber rafts (some of which took up to one hundred and fifty oarsmen per raft). Foreign immigrants entered the New World through Canada and Lake Champlain— "The Northern Gateway," as it was called—and several were stricken with cholera en route. Some died in the North Country and others stayed there to recuperate. Many of these immigrants were Irish, and they, with the French-Canadians, brought the first Catholic churches to the previously solid Protestant county. With cool confidence in unending supplies of timber, the settlers welcomed new signs of palpable civilization: newspapers, through highways, Masonic lodges, secondary schools, lawyers, doctors, politicians, and even a temperance movement. Only one disaster struck this lush postwar era—the infamous Cold Summer of 1816.

"Then came the summer which was no summer;/ But only a winter painted green," wrote a contemporary poet. All sorts of explanations were given for nature's peculiar estival performance that year. A prominent astronomer of the time offered the theory that planets in the same quarter of the heavens make disturbances through mutual attraction. *The Old Farmer's Almanac* said that the varying distance between the earth and the moon might influence the season. Others blamed it on sunspots, which, it was claimed, could be observed with the naked eye. Still oth-

ers said it was due to total eclipses of the sun and the moon in the spring of 1816. The most reasonable explanation was the cataclysmic eruption of a volcano in the East Indies, Mount Tambora, which sent clouds of dust into the stratosphere, effectively dimming the sun's rays throughout much of the Northern Hemisphere. Whatever the case, North Country people went hungry, a few nearly froze to death in June snowstorms, and some killed their starving cattle and then themselves, thinking it was the end of the world. Crops refused to grow, wells froze over, and a farmer could hire a carpenter for two weeks' work in return for just a couple of bushels of wheat or corn. Still, there were many instances of pioneer sharing and neighborliness, and there were always fish and game and wild berries to eat. Few actually starved to death, but it was two years before hay, wheat, rye, and corn flourished again and the birds returned to the Adirondacks.

In one of his more brilliant mercantile visions, William Gilliland foresaw, in 1783, the building of an "inland navigation from sea to sea," meaning from Lake Champlain to the Atlantic Ocean via the Hudson River. Of course, it was a route used by Indians for centuries, but they travelled in canoes and portaged much of the distance. If timber was to get to the hungry markets of Albany and New York City, then a canal big enough for immense lumber rafts would have to be dug. In 1823, the Champlain Canal—running from the southern tip of the lake at Whitehall to the Hudson River at Glens Falls—was completed

at a cost of less than one million dollars, and the lumber trade reached a new zenith. The lakeside hamlets of Port Kent, Essex, Westport, Port Henry, Crown Point, and Ticonderoga became bustling ports for canal boats, barges, rafts, schooners, sloops, and steamers. "It was not unusual," said a Westport navigator of the day, "to look out on our bay and see twenty sail at once." Not only did lumber move south now, but manufactured goods from the cities moved north, and everybody benefited. During the winters, powerful teams took over the shipping on the lake ice. Two years later, the Erie Canal, connecting Lake Erie with the Hudson, was finished and the canal-obsessed state legislature investigated the possibility of digging a waterway across the Adirondacks from Lake Champlain to Lake Ontario. (The legislature decided against this herculean scheme when its cost was estimated at a shocking two million dollars.) New York State soon was the nation's biggest lumber producer, with a billion board feet cut a year. Lake and canal piloting became an honorable, lucrative profession; steamboat captains were known to retire with as much as one hundred thousand dollars. A fruitful, if short-lived, industry was born, and almost every Essex lad suddenly had dreams of going to sea, as it were. Now, sad to say, only an occasional fuel barge or pleasure boat is seen on the lake. And the railroads that made the schooners and steamers obsolete are now almost obsolete themselves.

When the Papineau Rebellion broke out in Canada in 1837, there was genuine empathy among North Country

Americans for the patriots' cause against the British. Some Essex County men actually crossed the border to fight alongside the rebels, which alarmed President Van Buren enough so that he issued a proclamation forbidding any free-lance soldiering. Another war with England was certainly not desired by the President. A local offshoot of the doomed Canadian struggle occurred one day in 1838 when a group of young Elizabethtown hotbloods broke into the arsenal there and carried off twelve hundred muskets. The guns never made it to Canada; they were recovered the next day in a barn outside of the village. But the Spirit of 1776, and 1812, lingered on.

By the middle of the nineteenth century, it occurred to some that North Country timber was not limitless. New roads had opened up the inner wilderness to lumbermen, but promiscuous and wasteful cutting had left great irredeemable holes in the green tapestry. (One of the reasons American furniture of that period was so beautifully uniform was that lumbermen rarely bothered to take out of the forest any part of a tree above the first branch, thus eliminating knots and burls in the finished product.) Men with a wary eye to the future began to look into the ground instead of on top of it.

Every human being who had spent time in Essex County knew there was iron ore there, but few realized just how much until enormous ore beds were exposed in the town of Moriah. The proximity of the mines to Port Henry made the hauling of ore to the lake barges com-

paratively easy. Some far greater fortunes than the threatened lumber industry had ever produced were in the offing. This mineral bonanza—plus modern farming methods and the arrival of some adventurous tourists weary of the stagnation of Saratoga Springs—kept the North Country boom going. The population of Essex County swelled to a healthy thirty-one thousand, just thirty-six hundred short of what it is today.

One of the first financial coups made in the Adirondack wilderness was engineered by a trader of Dutch descent named Peter Smith, who skillfully cheated Indians out of valuable furs, which were sent on for resale to his New York City partner, John Jacob Astor. In the course of his dealings, Smith acquired about a million acres of New York land, including almost all of the town of North Elba, in Essex County. While he took a certain pleasure in evicting settlers from his property (always sending them on their way with a free copy of the Gospels), his son, Gerrit, was of a markedly different nature. A professional faddist and reformer, Gerrit soon tired of such tranquil crazes as vegetarianism and became active in the Underground Railroad for runaway slaves. In a burst of philanthropy, he made available, in 1846, much of his inherited land—a hundred and twenty thousand acres—to any Negroes who would clear and farm it. Smith's noble experiment offered a minimum of fifty free acres to each Negro family, and it attracted a lot of takers. A sizable all-black settlement—nicknamed Timbuctoo by the uneasy whites of the area—sprouted in the wilderness of North Elba, on

flatlands below Lake Placid, known as the Plains of Abraham. The whites needn't have been uneasy; as it turned out, the Negroes, mostly from the Deep South, couldn't stand the North Country winter and the difficult farming, and almost all of them left for warmer and more receptive climes by the end of the first year. The few who remained needed some inspired expertise if they were to make a go of the independent agrarian life, and Smith enlisted the aid of his fellow-abolitionist, John Brown.

Brown, a Yankee wool broker and cattle raiser, arrived at the Plains of Abraham in 1849, with his wife and several children. He bought from Smith for only a dollar an acre a two-hundred-and-forty-four-acre farm, which he planned to use as an example of productive agriculture for the Negroes. A New York State Agricultural Society report of 1850 referred to a "number of very choice and beautiful Devons from the herds of Mr. John Brown, residing in one of our most remote and secluded towns," but even with his personal success as an example, the experiment failed. As a consequence of this failure, Brown's abolitionist sentiments became severely militant. His older sons went off to homestead in Kansas, and Brown joined them there in 1855, organizing the wild raids on Kansas slaveholders that gained him notoriety all over America; meanwhile, his wife and younger children in North Elba were left practically penniless. On his trips back to Essex County, he agitated along the way for his cause and actually enlisted some North Country locals, white and black, in his private army. Once, he brought

back his grandfather's gravestone from Connecticut and set it behind his house near a huge rock. Possibly with a clear presentiment of what was in store for him, he announced that he wanted to be buried by that rock, and then carved his initials on it. In June, 1859, he left North Elba for Harpers Ferry, Virginia. By December, he was back in North Elba, under the ancient gravestone near the initialled boulder.

The return home of the hanged corpse of Essex County's most illustrious son, albeit adopted, was a moment of unexpectedly sincere sorrow for the citizens. The coffin arrived in Westport on December 6th, and a somber cortege accompanied it to Elizabethtown, where it lay in state in the County Court House. Six men stood vigil over it all night long, one of them riding off at dawn to inform the Brown family that "the old man" was coming home. Then the procession trudged through the cold mountains to North Elba and the final resting place near the great rock.

After the passions of the Civil War, which Brown himself had done so much to precipitate, had simmered down, the Brown farm and grave were violated by vandals and souvenir hunters. When the land was finally put up for sale, a Miss Kate Field formed the John Brown Society and managed to buy the property. Later, it was given to New York State, which restored the farmhouse, put the gravestone under a glass case, and reconstructed the barn from its original foundation. Today, where "John Brown's body lies a-molderin' in the grave" is a serene

and moving historical site few tourists ever bother to visit, although it is just outside Lake Placid. The farmhouse is a magnificent job of restoration. The simple furniture and implements are intact and there is an unusual sense of credulity about the place. And it is conforting to know that the surrounding view of the highest peaks the Adrondacks have to offer hasn't changed much in the last hundred years.

The men of Essex went to war again in 1861 to teach a lesson to "the misguided people of the Southern States," as one local partisan phrased it. They were all good Republicans and they all supported Lincoln. In fact, one of them, Congressman Orlando Kellogg of Elizabethtown, was an intimate friend of Lincoln. "If it was not for Kellogg's stories I should get blue sometimes," Lincoln once said during the height of the war. They were sympathetic to abolitionism, even to John Brown, although they feared any influx of Negroes and some had kept slaves up to a decade before the war. And, it must be added, the county paid generous bonuses for volunteers through its taxes, seven-per-cent bonds, and three-hundred-dollar draft-avoidance fees. Five companies were organized—not counting those who volunteered in Vermont units where the pay was a more munificent seven dollars a month—and the soldiers served in many famous battles, acquitting themselves well. The lesson-teaching cost the county about four hundred of its best men.

The postbellum period launched another golden age for Essex County, as it did for many other Northern

areas. Both the wood and the iron of the Adirondacks were in great demand throughout the expanding nation, and the unlimited water power of the strong rivers lured pulp and paper mills into the region. There were no restrictions; everything was up for grabs. Along with the lumber camps and the mining communities, new mill towns, with all their attendant dreariness, appeared almost overnight. Mills meant cheap labor, and cheap labor meant foreign immigrants. Italians, Germans, Eastern Europeans, and more French-Candians poured into the North Country. Unpronounceable names began to show up on voter lists among the Smiths and Straights and Dentons and Barretts, and while some were Anglicized, most retain their original spelling today.

Northern war money had created a new leisure class, and now more and more people were coming up to the North Country not to farm, mine, or cut trees but simply to relax in the mountains. At first, the only available hostelries—aside from the old Pavilion at Ticonderoga—were crude affairs, little more than extra space in an enterprising native's house. But by 1875 grand hotels and lodges in the Saratoga manner were being built in the most unlikely backwoods spots, offering lavish menus, no-limit, year-round hunting and fishing, and all kinds of sylvan adventure. Journalists and naturalists wrote extravagantly about the blessed life in the untamed wilderness. Suddenly the Adirondacks were fashionable. Stagecoaches, lake steamers, and the brand-new Delaware & Hudson and New York Central railroad lines brought

finely turned-out ladies and gentlemen to places that hadn't seen a lace cuff since the days of Fort St. Frédéric. The journey was called the Northern Grand Tour, and it had snob appeal; several of the *nouveaux riches* had already "seen" the Scottish Highlands, and the Adirondacks were supposed to be every bit as lovely and as chic. They were certainly much closer to home. The registers of the plush hotels sported such names as Astor, Stuyvesant, Vanderbilt, and Morgan. Ornate lodges were built and visited by Whitneys, Rockefellers, Harrimans, Lehmans, and Roosevelts. (Theodore Roosevelt learned of the shooting of President McKinley while he was enjoying the strenuous life at the Tahawus Club, in western Essex County, and he technically became President as he was being driven at breakneck speed through the mountains in the middle of the night by native teamsters. The momentous ride has naturally become a part of Adirondack lore, and a tablet honoring the event has been erected beside Route 28N, near Newcomb.) When word of the health-giving effects of mountain air got around, a whole new crop of visitors appeared—tuberculars. Soon sanatoriums were clustered around Saranac Lake and Bloomingdale, in the remote northwestern corner of the county, and miraculous cures for consumption were being publicized. Tourism, for relaxation or health, became a major industry. Hundreds of North Country people were employed as everything from guides to bellhops, and land values rose to an inflationary high. A few individuals and the *Times* expressed some doubt about whether the wil-

derness had any future as a wilderness, and meanwhile the money kept pleasantly rolling in.

North Country people, especially but not exclusively those over fifty, love to talk. Most of their talk is anecdotal and about the past. Recalling a person, a place, an incident, an emotion from some happier or sadder day has developed into a native craft, not just a device to escape the drag of winter or a tiresome chore. When one is introduced to an Essex County man, the how-do-you-do's are barely exchanged before the fellow will point to, say, a passing mongrel, which will remind him of the time old man Pierce from Minerva used to douse his yard with cayenne pepper to keep a pack of wild dogs away from his chickens. If one does not return the compliment with a comparable anecdote, the conversation is considered a failure and overt steps are taken to end it. While this protocol can be boring, its display of language and accuracy is admirable. There is deep pride of self, of neighbors, of idiom, and of region connected with the trait. Sometimes, it seems as if television had never been invented.

A man who remembers more than most about the banner postbellum period in Essex County's history, and who is more articulate than many men his age is Harry M. MacDougal, of Elizabethtown—Mr. Essex County. He was born in Elizabethtown in 1883, to a family that traced its Essex roots back to the seventeen-nineties. He doesn't look his years at all, and he is still active in Republican county politics. Slight and unassuming, he en-

joys sitting back, smoothing his thinning head of white hair, and remembering. He reminisced to a visitor one afternoon: "My mother had the t.b. when I was a boy. All the older people warned me to stay out of the house as much as possible. I was in school then, here in Elizabethtown. It was quite a place—an old iron-stove schoolhouse with an outside toilet. About two hundred kids walked through the snow for miles to get there. The teachers had whips and rubber hoses, and they knew how to use them. The lickings were something, all right, and there didn't have to be much reason to deal them out. Well, at about age twelve I had to quit school and take a job in a general store for fifteen dollars a month. Lifting things would build me up and keep me from the t.b., they told me. I did a lot of lifting. During the big timber boom at the turn of the century, I used to deliver groceries to the lumber camps, walking miles into the woods with those loads. My, it was exciting, though. Once a month, the lumberjacks—most of them were big Canucks—they'd get their pay and all hell'd break loose. There'd be eating and drinking like you wouldn't believe, and then the fighting —Oh, my, the fighting! I'm talking about free-for-alls. They'd take these terrible bloody beatings from each other, and then the next day they'd be at work, swinging an axe just like nothing. In the spring, there'd be river drives on the Boquet River to the pulp mill at Willsboro. The whole town would turn out to watch those fellows riding the big logs down the high river when they let the dams go. Every so often, one of them would get caught

between the logs and go in, and sometimes he wouldn't come up right away. Maybe never. But they were lumberjacks and they knew what life was like. The money was good, too, for the times. Some people complained about the land being stripped, but there were plenty of lumbering jobs, and a lot of cash was coming into town. The mining also brought in money, but there were ups and downs, just like nowadays. No welfare to speak of then, so the poor folks in Mineville froze and starved when the mines shut. The store owners would help by extending them as much credit as they could, but owing got the miners in worse trouble, it seemed. I remember the forge towns around here—Stower's Forge and New Russia. A couple of neighbors sitting on a little ore bed would decide to work it, doing their own smelting and selling the crude iron, and before you knew it they'd be calling the property Somebody-or-Other's Forge. A few of those places grew enough so they had a post office and a school, but they didn't last much past 1910, when they either ran out of ore or ran out of wood to fire their forges."

MacDougal saved his money and went to Albany Business College. (He is its oldest living alumnus.) Then he and his brother started their own grocery store, which thrived until the chain stores came along, in the 1920's. They sold out to the A. & P. chain, and MacDougal tried his hand at farming. "In the old days, the family farm got along pretty good," he said. "There were big families and plenty of sons, and the farmer grew most of his own food and had very little to buy. The farmers used to come into

my store and trade off their eggs, maple sugar, butter, and vegetables for stuff they couldn't grow. By the time I came around to farming, it had got harder to make a go of it. At one time, I had ten milkers, and I was president of the Dairymen's League, but, even so, I had to sell. Too small a return for the hard work. Now I walk around the valley and see the old abandoned farms—just a cellar hole is all that's left, really—and I feel lonesome. It pains me to see the old North Country farmer go.

"Well, anyway, when the tourists came in strong around here we used to have ourselves some real good laughs. Fancy ladies and their fancy gentlemen, dressed all wrong for the mosquitoes and black flies and the woods. They'd get off the stagecoach from the Westport railroad station with all their fancy luggage, and how we'd snicker! 'City boarders,' we called them. Of course, we knew they were laughing at us yokels, too, but that didn't prevent us from holding out our palms for their good money. It was what you might call a reciprocal relationship. When they were bored just sitting around on the verandas of the big hotels in town—the Deer's Head Inn and the Windsor—they'd take mountain tours with local guides, who told them all kinds of stories about man-eating bears and such. They brought in good money, but only from May to September. Then, in the twenties, people bought cars, and motor courts were built, and the old Windsor and the Deer's Head emptied out. They've torn them down since, and that's a shame. The tourists used to have some times in those places."

After giving up his farming, MacDougal discovered politics. In 1926, he was elected supervisor of Elizabethtown, and then county clerk. He was in and out of office until he retired, in 1965, but he is still honorary Republican County Chairman and works for various foundations, committees, and societies. He considers himself a Rockefeller Republican, but he loyally voted for Goldwater and for Nixon. "I don't think we can ever become a Democratic country," he said. "At least, I hope not. Republicanism is in the blood up here. But things change, the blood changes. Nowadays, politics comes out of the TV set—just so much toothpaste. I remember the old hot campaigns, like the one for Benjamin Harrison when I was a little fellow—the banners across Court Street, the bonfires, the parades, the fistfights, even. Teddy Roosevelt and Calvin Coolidge used to come up here, but nobody bothers with us anymore. They can reach us on the TV without travelling hundreds of miles to speak to just a handful of voters. People switch their loyalties now; they didn't then. It was all more fun in the old days."

AFTER the First World War, tourists found that Long Island and Cape Cod were the places to be seen at, and the great Adirondack hotels and millionaires' lodges went begging. The people who did pass through stayed in the motor courts and always seemed to be off the next morning for some other place. Summer camps for children helped the economy, and so did winter sports. Lake Placid benefitted from the sports more than any other town, and in 1932 it presented the Winter Olympics to several thousand hardy devotees. But the tourist business was on the wane.

As for the other industries the county relied on, the postwar news was not good. The Adirondack Forest Preserve had come into existence in 1885, and its regulations

were being strictly enforced. Timber-cutting operations were curtailed. The vast open-pit deposits of iron ore from the Mesabi Range, in Minnesota, were underselling the Essex ore in the American market. The family farm was dying. And the county's enclaves of heavy industry, the paper mills, were still making profits for their owners but were piling debt upon debt for the workers in the company towns.

Hubert Burrell, of Au Sable Forks (pronounced "Aw-SAY-bull," and variously written "Au Sable," "Ausable," or "AuSable"), was one of a small legion of North Country men who found a way out of the postwar economic bind: taking advantage of Essex County's proximity to Canada, he became a rumrunner. Now in his seventies, and white-haired and slowed by a heart condition, he is a long-inactive rumrunner as well as a retired papermill worker and deer hunter. There is the quality of the incurable rascal about him—mischievous eyes, white hair, Lyndon Johnson ears, a slyly humorous voice, and, in common with many other North Country patriarchs, a disarming openness.

"From the time I knew a deer from a horse, I could shoot good," he said one afternoon in his living room, a long stone's throw from the J. & J. Rogers paper mill. "But when I was in the Army, in the First World War, they sent me to the Argonne and I never had to fire a shot. That was O.K. with me. Deer for venison is all I ever wanted to shoot. I came home to Au Sable, but things weren't good here. Not much work around, and

what work there was you couldn't exactly call prosperous. I was itchy, so I bought myself an Overland coupe. Then came Prohibition. Me, the Overland, and Prohibition were made for each other. I heard about this little farm, just over the Canadian border, north of Mooers, that was a front for storing hooch. The barn and even the haystacks were filled with cases of the stuff. Well, I found out when the Border Patrol and the Mounties made their rounds, and soon I was running two quick trips a day from Au Sable, carrying cases of Johnnie Walker Red Label in the trunk. Twice a week, a man named Mr. Jones—how do you like that name?—he'd come up to Au Sable from New York City in a big Fiat with a chauffeur. A derby hat would be sitting on his head and a different woman on his lap every time. He'd haul about thirty cases of my Johnnie Walker back to the city. The woman, I suppose, made the eight-hour trip go faster. Anyway, that went on for one summer. I was making money, and so I decided to branch out a little. I bought myself a Buick roadster and a fast, heavy Cadillac, and I hired me some good drivers. We worked it this way: We cut out Mr. Jones—the middleman—and drove our stuff straight from Canada to a big bootlegger in Saratoga. One trip each day, seven days a week, twelve hundred dollars the trip. It was damn good money. We used the roadster as a pilot car, moving twelve miles ahead of me in the load car and keeping an eye out for the law. We usually took the back roads through the mountains as far as we could. The pilot car was supposed to double back if he spotted a

trap and warn me. One time, the pilot driver panicked when he saw a trap, and just kept going. Sure enough, the law stopped me, but I didn't desert the load until I could see the handcuffs on the trooper's belt. Then I ran into the woods and left my car. Had to walk all the way back to Au Sable through the mountains. I lost plenty of cars—five in a week once—but, you know, I was never caught. Some close calls, maybe, but I was never caught. Several of the others got nailed, though. One local boy was sent to Atlanta for a year and a day, but he didn't squeal on me. None of them did. They were good boys.

"Wait a minute, now. I was nailed once by a trooper, but I got the last laugh on him. You see, we used double springs on our cars so the heavy loads wouldn't drag down the rear end and give us away. Coming back empty to Au Sable, the rear end was always sticking way up in the air, so we put rocks in the trunk to keep it down. This trooper spotted me and pulled me over. He said, 'Let's see what's in your trunk.' I told him I lost the key, and he said, real smart-like, 'Well, I have a key right here that should fit,' and he jammed open the trunk with a crowbar. I just stood there laughing while he lifted out all the rocks. Then I told him if he'd put every rock back in the trunk nice and neat, I wouldn't make him pay for the damage he caused with the crowbar. He did just that and I drove off, as innocent as a fawn. Those cars we had were something, even for nowadays. You were always working while you drove—looking for the trap, moving the hand-operated windshield wipers, pumping up the

gas and oil pressure. We put armor plate behind the gas tank and a gadget for leaking oil onto the manifold to make a smoke screen. That's how we escaped the law a lot of times. They never could shoot out my tires. That's just in the movies. After a big snow, we'd sometimes use horse teams, but the troopers used to shoot the horses and we lost too many loads that way. Some troopers were on horses themselves, chasing us through the backroads. Real cowboys and Indians stuff. There was trouble with highjackers later on. They'd pretend to be the law, only they didn't fool me. Just drove right at them and watched the punks scatter. Most highjackers, they were Italians from up here. The Italians had a big bootlegging operation going with their own garages and cars and sources. I tried to stay clear of them. They had a way of talking too much."

Because of the efforts of Burrell and his colleagues, Au Sable Forks was suddenly blessed with a thriving new industry. As a busy rumrunning center, the small riverside village saw more loose cash than it had ever seen before or since. "Ah, the money!" Burrell continued, his spirits lifted by the mere thought of it. "Everyone in town knew what was going on but nobody squealed because they were all getting a slice of the pie. For instance, you take the garages. Now I alone was one hell of a customer. Not only did I buy a mess of cars but I spent a fortune for repairs. They used to charge me a hundred and twenty-five dollars just to replace a Cadillac timing chain. Had me over the old barrel, you know. And the fake registrations

cost, too. I had to pay ten dollars a week to a farmer just so I could use a back road on his property. I never bribed the law but others did. They told me I could do all the business I wanted for five hundred a week in the right palms. Most of the law was honest, though. My neighbor down the street here was a federal agent. He used to chase me during the day and then we'd play poker together at night. I took hundreds off him and some others. Those poker games! You could lose five hundred in half an hour. All the bootleggers gambled big, and drank, too —but never on the job. We forever had these thick wads of cash on us and sometimes I had about twenty thousand dollars around the house in jars and things. Careless? Why, once I was being chased and this thick wad in my back pocket was making me uncomfortable, so I just took it out and threw it on the seat beside me. Then I wrecked the car and forgot all about the wad when I ran off into the woods. What I wouldn't give just to *see* that wad today. Yes sir. I wasn't married then, and it was easy money. Easy come, easy go."

Burrell remained prosperous during the first two years of the Depression, but by 1932 his luck was running out, and he was down to his last car, a Model T. "It quit on me one day," he said. "I had to leave it with the load still inside. After that, I didn't have enough cash left to buy myself a pack of cigarettes. In the end, crime don't pay, I guess, but it sure was a hell of a lot of laughs. The whole county was out of work then. I got a job, though, working on the roads. A dollar-fifty a day. Christ, that's what I

used to tip a counterman in a diner for a cup of coffee so he'd keep his mouth shut. Well, anyhow, things were rough. I worked as a caretaker for a millionaire's camp down at Loon Lake, and then I was hired by the J. & J. Rogers Paper Company, here in Au Sable, to work in the beater room. The Rogers people ran a real company town in those days. 'The Robbers,' I called them. You sweated seven days a week back then for thirteen dollars, and one-seventy-five of that was taken out for rent. We all owed our souls to the credit corporation. We ended up slaving for practically nothing. But during the Second World War some C.I.O. organizers got ahold of me and made me the first union worker here. In no time at all, we had almost all the five hundred employees unionized. I was fired, but the union demanded that they hire me back, and they did, to my amazement. When the company won a pile of war contracts, we went out on a one-day strike. Mr. Chahoon—he was running the mill then—said he'd shut down and lock us out. But Morello, this organizer from the city—he threatened to have the government come in and take over the plant, which they could do in wartime. Morello threatened to phone Washington right from Chahoon's office, and Chahoon backed down. We won a ten-cent-an-hour raise and, later on, vacation and health insurance and pensions. You'd think they gave us Santa Claus, the way they carried on. Ten years ago or so, the mill was sold to a new outfit, and there was a long strike. People left town, and those that stayed barely made out. Finally, the workers accepted a pay cut, and

the mill opened again. I was retired then, and the new company fought me on my pension. I got me a lawyer, and he won back fifty per cent of it. That and Army benefits and Social Security is what I live off of. I still haven't enough to buy all the cigarettes I'd like. Robert Kennedy got the mill some government contracts while he was senator, but when the profit from them goes I don't know what will happen to the mill. They're running through the hardwood too fast, and also, under state law, they got to end their pollution of the Ausable River in 1971. That's expensive. When the mill closes, it'll be the end of this town. Au Sable will be just another Adirondack ghost town. And there won't be any love lost for the mill owners, I can tell you that." As Burrell predicted, the mill closed permanently in the spring of 1971.

In good times or bad, Burrell always hunted deer in the mountains around the Ausable Valley. He and several other men of different callings, including a writer and a book publisher from New York City, have a campsite in the Adirondack Forest Preserve where they get together every November to hunt, drink bourbon, swap stories, and relax. "There aren't many trees up here I haven't walked by," Burrell said. "I've been hunting pretty near all my life. Shot close to a thousand deer and six bear. Always ate the venison. I can't understand people who kill and don't eat the venison. City fellows, mostly. Some of them would offer to buy our dead deer so they'd have a trophy to show at home. They'd get too cold in camp and give up. Most people up here depend on venison for a lot

of their meat, believe it or not. Not many people eat bear meat, but during the hard times we'd auction off the skins to hotel guests, who'd make rugs from them. I'm set against jack-lighting, but I have nothing against poaching. I used to poach the Whitney and Rockefeller estates years ago. I figured they had too much anyway, and wouldn't miss a few bucks." Burrell laughed at his joke. "I took some deer right outside the caretakers' houses. Then I'd hide the carcasses under leaves and pick them up the next day. Then, last fall, bad heart and all, I went up to camp with my old Savage rifle and the best of intentions. I walked a little in the woods, and I got tired and sat down on a fallen tree. A nice deer came upwind of me and stood there in a clearing. It was an easy shot, but I missed. It depressed me, so I decided to stay in camp and just wash dishes and bring in wood for my friends. That's all I'm good for now—washing dishes. I don't think I'll go hunting anymore."

In mid-1961, the federal government officially declared Essex County a depressed area. The county leaders and the citizens had claimed for decades that the area was depressed, but the federal government moves in strange ways. Its criterion for defining a depressed area is based on unemployment figures from the Labor Department—or, as they put it in Washington, "substantial and persistent labor surplus." The Republic Steel Corporation's iron-ore mines in Mineville had shut down in June of 1960, in one of their longer periodic closings, and by the

time they reopened for partial production, late in 1961, unemployment had risen to almost twelve per cent of the county's working population. To make matters worse, a pulp-and-paper mill at Willsboro closed, putting about two hundred more workers out of jobs. By late 1961, eight hundred and forty-nine unemployment-insurance claimants had exhausted their benefit rights. Satellite stores and businesses around the one-industry towns were losing money, welfare rolls were growing, and tax revenues were dwindling. Workers' families lucky enough to live in trailers were packing up and moving on to where the jobs seemed to be—to the South and West. It was clear that at last the proud North Country men of Essex County would have to accept some substantial outside aid.

Under the Area Redevelopment Act of 1961, designed primarily to treat the chronic economic ills of Appalachia and similarly blighted regions, federal funds were made available to declared depressed areas for industrial and commercial projects, public facilities, and occupational training—that is, to keep the industry already in the county going and to bring new industry to the area. The Essex County Development Corporation was formed out of an initial grant of four thousand dollars from the county's Board of Supervisors. In 1968, this project expanded to include four neighboring North Country counties, under the name of the Eastern Adirondack Economic Development Commission. Its executive director, Karl Hofmann, of Port Henry, is a rare local example of contempo-

rary success. The son of a railroad worker, Hofmann worked his way through Middlebury College, in Vermont, and earned a Ph.D. in organic chemistry at Rensselaer Polytechnic Institute. Then he started a laboratory in Port Henry for extracting hormones from pregnant mares' urine (which was shipped to Essex County in tank cars, creating quite a stir in railroad circles), and from 1948 to 1955 his little laboratory manufactured a large percentage of the natural steroids used in America. After the advent of artificially produced steroids in 1955, he sold his business, and since then he has devoted most of his time to trying to solve the seemingly insoluble problems of the area.

"The Development Corporation and later the Commission have come up with over six million dollars from federal and state funds since 1961," Hofmann said to a visitor in his office, which overlooks the Port Henry railroad yards—a bleak expanse of empty, rusting ore cars. "Some of that money went to build the Uihlein Mercy Center, in Lake Placid—a nonsectarian extended-care facility run by the Sisters of Mercy. It's a place for sick old people, and it has also created some fulltime jobs in the Lake Placid district. Then, we raised half a million for an addition to the Lake Placid Olympic Arena, and that is already paying off with conventions and sports attractions throughout the year. We've contributed to village water and sewage projects to improve Lake Champlain for tourism, and we've helped attract some home-grown small industry, from a frozen-pizza company in Ticonderoga to a

tiny plastics outfit near Westport. But all this is just a drop in the bucket—a few permanent jobs here and there. Of course, this past year Essex County lost the J. & J. Rogers paper mill in Au Sable Forks and the Republic Steel operation at Mineville, so we're not even holding our own anymore. One big trouble is the same as it is in most parts of Appalachia: there's no real future for the young people. They look around and see the sad state the local economy is in, see their fathers on relief, their mothers getting old before their time, and they say, 'This isn't for me.' The young leave the county any way they can—through the armed services (we've had a disproportionate number of boys in Vietnam), through jobs in the cities, through vocational–education opportunities in other places—and they don't plan on coming back here until they're ready to retire. The funny thing is, the kids love living here. The mountains and the trees and the rivers are in the blood. They all know how to hunt and fish and live outdoors. But they just have to get away, if they're going to survive in the technological world."

The result of this exodus of the young has been a decrease in the county's population since the 1960 census—a period in which the population of almost all the other counties in New York State has increased. (At present, the population density of Essex County is about nineteen people to a square mile, the third lowest in the state. There are as many persons in one average square mile of Brooklyn as there are in all 1,823 square miles of Essex County.) "Most of the people who are left here are get-

ting on in years, or they're retired folks who come here to live out their lives in quiet surroundings close to nature," Hofmann continued. "What we need to revitalize the area for younger working people is an industrial park with light, clean industry, like the kind they have around Boston—electronic parts and that sort of thing. We are currently building an industrial park in Plattsburgh which may provide jobs for some commuters from Essex County. And under the Emergency Employment Act passed last summer, Essex County got a hundred and forty thousand dollars in federal funds, to be used in creating new jobs. But if the general economic trend keeps up, there won't be *anybody* needed here but a few caretakers for the tourists. A vocational-training center would help. If we could show industry that we have a ready supply of trained young people, industry might give us a second thought. It's happening right across the lake in Vermont—I.B.M. and General Electric are in Burlington, and Simmonds Precision has a plant in Vergennes—so why not here? It's the same climate and the same kind of people. We've even got the Northway now. Maybe we could reestablish Lake Champlain as a transportation route, using hydrofoils or fast barges, or build an airport for industry. Well, those are nice dreams, anyway. When I used to go down to Washington, as head of the Essex County Development Corporation, I told them about what we need to survive in Essex County. But I used to get the feeling that Washington never really understood what went wrong with our old industries."

Each of the old industries has its own mercurial history. Farming, the earliest and most basic of them, has had one of the most catastrophic, which is true in so much of rural America. As recently as 1930, there were 1,757 farms in Essex County. Today, there are about three hundred, and half of these are commercial—that is, large farms with produce sales of twenty-five hundred dollars a year or more, and not necessarily owned by a resident. The result is that the classic, primarily self-sufficient American family farm—that prevailing symbol of the Sticks for city dwellers—is disappearing from the land.

Wilford R. Crowningshield, who lives in the hamlet of Deerhead, near Elizabethtown, is in both looks and destiny the model of a North Country farmer—jutting jaw, chiselled face, gnarled, honest hands, and a discouraged demeanor brightened by a hint of peasant sharpness. "Back in 1920, my father and uncles had three farms hereabouts," Crowningshield told a friend not long ago. "They were mostly dairy, but we had some crops, too. Eight hundred acres, all told, and most of it good pasture land. The people called the area Crowningshield, after our property. We all worked the place—us children, my mother, my aunts, everybody. In the winter, we cut wood to help pay the taxes, and, what with all hands pitching in, we made a go of it. We were no millionaires, but we ate regular and enjoyed it. Then, in the thirties, my father and uncles, they got old and died, and I was left with the properties. Even though the family was still

pitching in to help—I have six children myself—there seemed to be more work and less money coming in. For instance, the milk trucks always used to come right to the barns to collect the milk. It was just a matter of course. Well, the truck operators told me they couldn't afford to do that anymore, and I'd have to bring my milk to them at a collection point in town. That took a lot of time I didn't have to spare. I couldn't do it all myself, and I couldn't hire help. To make ends meet, I tried planting alfalfa, but the soil's too sandy for alfalfa. I had to earn extra income somehow, so I drove a school bus for the Elizabethtown schools and tried to keep the farm going at the same time. Finally, in 1948, I gave up farming for good. There was just no sense in it anymore. I sold out two of the farms and got myself a full-time job as janitor for the schools. My wife died and the children are all grown now, but I still live in one of the farmhouses, and keep a little garden there, just to remind me. An old woman lives alone in another of the farmhouses, and the third one has all gone to brush. I can't complain about the janitor's job. The people I work for are good, and I'm retiring soon with a pension, but I sure miss the old ways. I loved farming—the stock, the horses, growing most of your own food, hunting and fishing on your own land. The milk prices could ruin you overnight, but at least you were your own boss. I liked that. But what can you do? Can't pass a losing proposition on to your young. Of my six children, four are already out of the county—one is a radar-equipment repairman over in Belgium. There's not

much to keep them here."

Ray Bender is a salty gentleman who has won a certain fame throughout the county both as "a character" and as "the farmer's savior." For twenty-seven years, he was the county agent—the local representative of the federal and state Departments of Agriculture, whose job is to counsel and occasionally browbeat farmers into accepting the fruits of scientific research. He was also a town supervisor in Westport. Now, having retired, he is a columnist for the Plattsburgh *Press-Republican* and an observer of life from his home, a comfortable house overlooking Lake Champlain. The coup of his career as county agent was his introduction to the hard-pressed Champlain Valley farmers of a profitable feed crop called bird's-foot trefoil, a bright-yellow plant whose ripe pods when held upside down resemble the spread toes of a bird. "I got the idea of experimenting with this stuff in 1936," Bender said not long ago while fondling a sample of the plant he had found growing wild in his front yard. "I had a hunch it would grow in the light upland soil of the Champlain Valley, where other feed crops, like alfalfa, have a hard time. I planted inoculated seed on one acre in each of five different farms around here, and, sure enough, the damn thing grew like all getout. It turned out to be just as successful in the clay soil down near the lake. We found that cattle love to eat it, that it won't cause bloat in their paunch, the way other feeds sometimes will, and that the plant persists year after year. Cattle can damn near explode with the bloat. What we do here is grow the stuff

and then wait till the pods become ripe, in August. We harvest the pods and sell them to cattle raisers for their own pastures. Now, when those pods get too dry, they pop open and eject the seeds, so the harvesting is kind of tricky. You've only got a few days' leeway or you lose all your seeds. We have a cooperative with our own combines—special threshers—and seed-processing plant, and we help each other out with staggered harvesting to catch the seeds while they're still in the pods. Essex County is now one of the largest producers of bird's-foot trefoil in the world. That may not win us any prizes, but it has made some money for farmers around these parts just when they were on the skids. Canada is producing the seed now, so the demand is easing off. That's how it goes in farming.

"Oh, we got troubles, all right. There are the natural ones of the weather, the soil, the short growing season, the stones that keep turning up again after you break your back pulling them out. Stones always seem to grow well. And, don't forget, much of the county is vertical real estate, and state-owned at that. Only about ten per cent of the land is usable for agriculture. Then, we have a scarcity of experienced agriculture labor, even if a farmer is rich enough to hire somebody. Labor these days is taking out more than it's putting in. We're pricing ourselves right out of the market. Kids can't even work on farms in the summers anymore, because of the laws—minimum wage and all. Of course, it's better and cheaper to have good, strong sons, but most sons don't want to farm now-

adays. They cut out of the county for an easier, more secure life. So the trend here is toward merging, just like your big companies—fewer farms but bigger ones, more machinery, more experts. Dairy and feed crops work best in this county, but they can be pretty chancy. The old chicken-and-potato farmer—he's gone for good. Even the farmers' houses are going—to decay or to the summer people. The old-style ornery, independent hay-kicker is dying off, and personally I'm damned sorry about it. I was no white-shirt county agent. I dressed and acted just like one of the hay-kickers—never knocked on a door, just went inside and yelled. I really hate to see the likes of us disappear."

If it is difficult to find a practicing farmer in Essex County today, it is harder still to find a professional lumberman. Woodcutters are hired on a part-time basis for such odd jobs as felling stands of likely and unlikely pine on private property, clearing trees and brush for highway construction, cutting down cedars for a small fence-post factory, and supplying hardwood pulp for the one surviving paper mill. But the burly lumberjack of the golden timber era has all but vanished. There are just eight sawmills operating full time in the county, where there were hundreds a century ago, and these mills do not always use native wood. What little commercial timbering that remains on private land is done by a few men with power tools and tractors; the massive, vapor-snorting lumbercamp horses that once dragged great logs from the woods

are seen only at the county fair, pulling concrete-laden sleds for prize money.

The timber industry in Essex County—the region's first treasure—declined through a perverse combination of lack of foresight and an abundance of it. After the Revolutionary War, the embryonic State of New York held vast wildernesses that had belonged first to the Iroquois and then to England. The state reasoned, with the enviable naïveté of the times, that if these tracts were privately owned they would produce tax revenues, and private ownership would also cure a gigantic real-estate headache. Consequently, much of the land passed into private hands, at prices as low as five cents an acre. The land buyers, whose roster included some of the most distinguished names in the nation, speculated with their bargains until it became clear that the big money was in the timber on the land. The land barons turned into lumber barons. Their usual practice was to strip the land of every tree over ten feet tall and then deliberately not pay taxes, so that the useless, wasted acreage would revert to the state. The great white pine went first, for ships' masts and spars as well as lumber, and then the spruce, which was ideal for pulp. Timber thieves—known by such sobriquets as "The Grenadiers" and "The State Troopers"—invaded the forests, taking choice timber from property that the state still held and burning the rest to mask their raids. Railroads came into the wilderness to haul out the timber, bringing smokestack sparks, and the ensuing forest fires feasted on the debris left by the lumbermen. Both

the settlers and the wildlife suffered. Then a dedicated Adirondack surveyor, Verplanck Colvin, alerted the state legislature to the situation, and at last, toward the end of the nineteenth century, some action was taken to ease the problem.

In 1885, the embarrassed legislature created the Adirondack Forest Preserve, through a law that present and future state land "shall be forever kept as wild forest lands" and "shall not be sold nor leased or taken by any person, corporation, public or private." However, the law didn't mention the trees on this preserved land. The rape of the forests went on within the boundaries of the Preserve. In 1892, the Adirondack Park—an area in which the state intended to concentrate its purchases of forest land—was formed, and its boundaries were marked on state maps with a blue line. (The state actually owned and controlled only a quarter of the land within the blue line; the rest belonged to private landholders. Today it owns thirty-eight per cent.) Two years later, conservationists pushed through a provision at the Constitutional Convention of 1894, making the original law part of the state constitution and adding these words: ". . . nor shall the timber thereon be sold, removed, or destroyed." The fact that this law was now a part of the state constitution protected the issue from the whims and dealings of shady legislators. The state found itself buying back some of its old nickel-an-acre land for more than ten times the price it had sold for, and certain parcels went for as much as fourteen dollars an acre. The sanctity of the Preserve was

strictly enforced by the newly formed Forest Commission, and what remained of the woods was saved from the lumber barons. Since 1900, however, uncontested decisions by state attorneys general and the passage of constitutional amendments have violated the purist spirit of the "forever-wild" provision; for instance, public campsites were cleared in the Preserve, ski trails and a highway were authorized for Whiteface Mountain, and the Northway was constructed through Preserve land in the south of Essex County. These incursions (and there are others, still in the planning stage) have caused a deep, bitter rift between commercial-minded people, who think that the Adirondack Forest Preserve is a waste of good land, and "forever-wilders," who think that the Preserve should be just that—an untouchable, untouched sanctuary, eternally free of the inroads of civilization. The New York State Department of Environmental Conservation suffers the abuse of both groups.

"I can see the point of the lumbermen and the others who want to prune out some trees and manage the Preserve," a senior forester at one of the Department's Adirondack headquarters said not long ago in his office outside Lake Placid. "Good managing would clear away a lot of potential fire hazards, help smaller trees to grow, provide more food for wildlife, and bring in some money for the state. What many folks are afraid of, though, is that Preserve forest managing would be difficult to control. Lumbermen would take out more than they should from state land, and there goes the forest. I believe in the

forever-wild idea, and I believe recreation comes before timbering—which is to say I believe in the status quo. Laurance Rockefeller's proposal to make a national park out of the high-peaks area of the Preserve has been shelved, I gather. There was the question of damming the Hudson River near Newcomb for a reservoir, which would have inundated a lot of Preserve land and a good part of the town land. I suppose there are arguments for projects like this, but I wonder what will be left of the Preserve if bits and pieces keep getting chipped off. A dam here, a road there—it all adds up.

"People from all over love the Preserve. It may have hurt the timber industry, but it brought in millions of tourists. And, don't forget, the state pays its own way; it coughs up town and county tax money just like any other property owner. Some of the poorer towns around here would be dead broke if it weren't for the state land-tax money coming in. Our forest rangers—twelve in Essex County alone—help out the communities with rescue work and firefighting and woods maintenance. Of course, we're rough on timber thieves and game butchers. The penalty for cutting a tree on state-owned Preserve land could be as much as a hundred dollars plus three times the value of the tree. But over the long run both the locals and the tourists are pretty honest. Litter and trash are problems, what with plastic and aluminum containers for everything these days. You should see some of those campsites on an August Monday morning."

He walked over to a large wall map of the Adirondack

Park on which the Forest Preserve land was marked in a pink crazy-quilt pattern. "We're adding acreage all the time," he said. "But it's mostly in small parcels, which is why the map looks as if it had the measles. We receive some land gifts from conservation-minded citizens, but what we buy comes from broke farmers and used-up mill lands. We take good care of what we have—watching for fires, reforesting wherever we can, fighting tree diseases and insects. It's quite a thing, this preserved wilderness—really one of a kind, for a state to operate all by itself. The people, especially from the cities, they need something like this—something that's still a forest primeval, free of pollution and machines and noise. It's worth keeping that way." Last June, the Adirondack Park Agency was voted into existence as a regulatory body for dealing with land use in an increasingly macadamized area. Everyone agrees it will have its collective hands full.

Just as Essex County timber was in extravagant supply when it was most needed by a burgeoning nation, rich deposits of iron ore were also discovered at precisely the right time. The fortunes amassed from iron made the timber killings look like a schoolboy's allowance. The Iroquois had long known how to fashion crude implements from the iron-bearing rock found all over the region, and, with typical generosity, they had shown the outcroppings to the first whites. Gilliland and Skene knew about the ore near Lake Champlain, and Benedict Arnold noted in his 1775 diary that he had "sent a boat with Skene's ne-

groes to dig ore" near Port Henry for smelting and forging into cannon balls to hurl against the British. Fortuitous mineral strikes were common in the region during the pioneer years. In 1815, a Ticonderogan named Charles Wood was tending his cattle one day when he happened to hit some moss with a hatchet. The cut in the moss exposed a deep vein of high-quality graphite, which until twenty-five years ago was used in pencils trademarked "Ticonderoga." Another man discovered several chunks of ore above ground. He dug, found more, and was advised by a friend, according to a published report of the find, "You needn't dig any more there. It is contrary to philosophy. This ore must have come from above." Forges and rolling mills sprouted here and there in the North Country. One of the first American blast furnaces was built at Port Henry, in 1822. Hundreds of men, including many Italians and Poles, became miners or smelters, but they saw very little of the money that was made from their work. The profits went to the gentlemen of Wall Street, who were quick to explore and possess the area. By 1880, Essex County and Clinton County were supplying almost a quarter of all the iron ore mined in the United States.

The best deposits were in the small mountains northwest of Port Henry. A pair of dingy mining villages called Witherbee and Mineville, which sit over three deep ore beds, look for all the world like Welsh mining towns, complete with threatening tips of tailings, a few seedy, unpainted stores and taverns, an oppressive grayness in

faces and things, and a rambling cemetery filled with consonantal names almost too long for the gravestones. The ore there is high-grade magnetite, which in its pure form is about seventy-two per cent iron; only some Swedish magnetite is richer than the Mineville variety. (The superior iron made from this magnetite was chosen during the Civil War to sheathe the *Monitor.*) The Republic Steel Corporation took over the mines in 1938, and began using the Mineville magnetite to enrich the poorer but more plentiful ore from Minnesota and Michigan in its own steelmaking ventures. This procedure has had its ups and downs through the years.

In August, 1968, the one working mine in the area closed for the month's vacation that was allotted to the four hundred and thirty employees, and it didn't open again until February 4, 1969, when it was announced that there would be no overtime work. During the long lull, the Republic Steel executives, in cheerless metallic offices near the mines, refused to give any hint about the future of operations there, but the laid-off miners, sitting around the dismal Port Henry bars, killed their afternoons exchanging rumors. On a chilly, rainy late-summer day after it was announced that the 1968 vacation would be extended indefinitely, one of the miners—Stanley, as he will be called—nursed his Genesee beer and discussed his unpromising trade. "A fellow on the maintenance crew was just telling me that we'll be working again after Christmas," Stanley said. "But I don't know—you hear so many stories. The best thing is to wait and see. You learn

that when you've been mining long enough. The younger fellows get restless and jump with every story. But fellows like me who've been around and remember the big shutdown of 1961—we just sit tight and try to make do. The union will help us out, and then there's unemployment compensation, and, if things get real tough, county welfare." Stanley spat out the last two words. "People wonder why we don't move on to where the steady jobs are," he went on. "Well, I'll tell you. There's good money in mining since the union and when things are humming. A lot of us make over two hundred a week and get some nice fringe benefits besides. That's big money up here. Most of us own the houses we live in—bought them at a good price from the company. We got roots here, and we all like the area—the outdoors, the hunting, the ice fishing on the lake. We made a good contract with the company. But even more than that is—it's kind of hard to say—the *satisfaction,* I guess you'd call it, of being a miner. When you come up out of the shafts after a day's work, you feel like a man—like you did something. It's dangerous down there—we lose people once in a while—but that makes you feel better yourself for coming through."

Stanley's face reddened slightly, and he finished his beer and continued, "The reason the mine is having a bad time is the engineers aren't exploring any new beds. When the iron formed around here, millions of years ago, it spread out underground like sort of fingers. Well, for over a hundred years now we've been blasting ore, which has been just dandy, but now they're beginning to run

out of the stuff. The company has got to blast out over a million tons a year to break even. There are still huge pillars of pure ore down there for the taking, but if we cut those what's going to hold up the mine? The company would rather cut production than touch those pillars. What with the big ore finds in Labrador, I'm afraid this mine will die sooner or later. It's too expensive for the big boys in the Cleveland home office, I guess."

Stanley ordered another beer. "If we never open again, I don't know what will happen to the younger fellows," he said. "Maybe they'll get work at the new paper plant in Ti, maybe they'll work on the road, maybe they'll pack up and move on. But they won't be miners, and that's a shame. I got enough time in so I can afford to sit out the layoff and stay with mining. There's a pension coming to me, and the Social Security, one day. I guess I'll just sit it out." Since last July, Stanley and his co-workers have been doing a lot more sitting, or they have moved on. All mining operations have again been indefinitely halted at Mineville and Witherbee. A Meals on Wheels program—providing hot, nutritious food at little or no cost to poverty-stricken families still living in the area—is currently rolling through the streets of the depressed villages.

A qualified success story of Essex County mining is in Tahawus (locally pronounced "TA-HAWS"), a churning industrial speck in the wilderness just southwest of Mount Marcy and the primary source of the Hudson River, Lake Tear of the Clouds. There, twenty-four hours a day, NL Industries (formerly the National Lead Company) mines

one of the world's largest producing deposits of precious ilmenite titanium ore, which is used to make pigments for paper, paint, ceramics, and rubber. Contentment was once the rule in isolated Tahawus; however, from August, 1971, to January, 1972, the two hundred or so employees were on strike. Because of a new production process developed during the strike, only eighty-two men were invited back to work in January. The rest, of course, are on welfare. This was by no means the only crisis Tahawus has weathered through the years.

At the beginning of the nineteenth century, Archibald McIntyre, the owner of an unprofitable iron furnace in North Elba, sent his son John with Duncan McMartin, Jr., a business partner, and David Henderson, an ambitious engineer, to prospect for silver in the high peaks of the Adirondacks. By all accounts, a Canadian Indian mysteriously appeared one day and showed a piece of iron ore to Henderson. "You want to see 'um ore, me fine plenty—all same," the Indian was quoted as saying. "Me hunt beaver all 'lone, and fine 'um where water run over iron dam." For a dollar and fifty cents and a bit of tobacco, this central-casting Indian led the party to an "iron dam" at the then unknown headwaters of the Hudson—actually, a ledge of iron ore across a stream. The prospectors realized that the ledge must be an outcrop of an inestimable ore deposit, and hastened to Albany, where they bought more than a hundred thousand acres of the area from the state at ten cents an acre. (On the way, Henderson bought a lottery ticket that later won

him five hundred dollars. "I am afraid," he wrote, "I am getting too lucky in this way to be lucky in other matters." Several years later, Henderson went off into the mountains to search for new sources of water power. While removing his pistol belt, he accidentally discharged his gun and critically wounded himself. He died by a little lake now known as Calamity Pond. The luck he was so suspicious of had indeed run out.) Under Archibald McIntyre's aegis, they formed the Adirondac Iron & Steel Co., and for a while their little industry in the woods flourished. They tried all sorts of experimental methods for smelting iron into steel, and by the 1850's they had founded two communities—Adirondac and Tahawus (the latter name taken from the Senecan "He splits the sky," supposedly referring to Mount Marcy). Adirondac had a population of four hundred, a bank, and a school. Tahawus was a smaller village. There was a rough wagon road through the forest to Lake Champlain. Apart from the problem of hauling iron some forty miles by wagon to the lake, there was the vexing matter of an odd, heat-resistant impurity that made the iron difficult to work with and caused a lot of customer complaints. The impurity had been identified as titanium, but at the time nobody could figure out a practical use for it. Luck began to run out for the adventurous company. Rampaging floods, financial panic, and the nuisance of the titanium soon turned Adirondac and Tahawus into ghost towns. Adirondac was later acquired by some wealthy sportsmen and became the Tahawus Club, on whose rustic premises

Theodore Roosevelt learned that McKinley was dying. But for the most part the once bustling industrial complex reverted to bush.

A practical use for titanium was finally discovered—a process that converted this blackest of minerals into the whitest of pigments. For many years, however, Norway and India supplied all the raw titanium that American industry wanted. Then the Second World War put a sudden end to that supply. Titanium was urgently needed by the armed forces—as a smoke-screen chemical, among other things—and in 1941 the government gave high priority to the National Lead Company to reactivate Tahawus and extract ilmenite from the iron ore there. A highway, bridges, electric-power lines, and processing plants were hastily constructed, and fifteen months later Tahawus was alive again—with a population of eight hundred. Since then, two more vast transformations have visited Tahawus. In 1953, Sanford Lake—actually a widening of the Hudson River as it rushes out of the mountains—was filled in with tailings, and the Hudson was rerouted through a man-made canal. (The NL Industries executives at Tahawus claim proudly that they've been able to keep their part of the river free of pollution, despite the industrial activity on its banks.) Ten years later, the company decided to obliterate the workers' village of Tahawus, because it was sitting right on top of an extremely valuable ore bed. Rather than build another community from scratch, National Lead literally moved the entire village to Newcomb, twelve miles away.

Houses, apartment buildings, a store, and two churches were hoisted onto gigantic flatbed trailer trucks and hauled to the newly prepared site. It is generally accepted by the natives that the "village move," as it is called, was the most extraordinary thing that has ever happened in Essex County, Joe Call's feats of strength and Rogers's escape from the Indians notwithstanding. Today, a Texaco station is all that is left of the old Tahawus. As for Adirondac, it has become a ghost town again, poked through by summer hikers on their way up trails to Mount Marcy.

Another qualified success story in Essex County mining concerns a fibrous, talc-like mineral called wollastonite. The Essex town of Willsboro has the only commercial source of wollastonite in the nation, and while this may seem to be a heaven-sent economic blessing, there are, unfortunately, very few commercial uses for the mineral. That sort of situation is stoically accepted as just another example of North Country luck.

The man responsible for whatever value wollastonite has at present is a gracious, pipe-smoking geologist, mining engineer, and county elder named Koert D. Burnham. Burnham became interested in the possibilities of wollastonite in 1936, through his father, a much admired creative man who was an intimate of John Burroughs, Thomas Edison, and Henry Ford. "My father was full of wild, idealistic notions," Burnham told a friend not long ago. "Like building inexpensive log cabins that an earthquake couldn't budge, and maintaining his own deer-

breeding preserve, and using different Essex County towns along Lake Champlain as assembly-line stops for manufacturing Ford automobiles. Henry Ford thought a lot of that last idea back in 1915, but it didn't pan out. What a pity! We would've been one big Detroit here. Maybe it's not such a pity after all. Anyway, my father saw a future for wollastonite. I got a grant to explore its potential. I had studied geology at Columbia, and naturally I became fascinated with the stuff myself. We discovered that the needlelike fibres of wollastonite crisscross to form natural lamination, and therefore could be used to make extra tough molds and cement." Burnham opened a desk drawer and brought out a six-inch strip of cement mixed with wollastonite. He tried to break the strip with his hands until his face was almost the color of his red-flannel shirt. "You see," he said. "You can't crack this compound unless you use a hammer. Great rupture strength. Also, it has some of the properties of asbestos, and you can use it for insulation, nose cones, ceramic ball bearings—in fact, ceramics of all kinds. We've assigned some money to Alfred University, over in the southwestern part of the state, for ceramic research on wollastonite. Something can be done, too, with garnets, which are a by-product of wollastonite refining. But so far we're still waiting for the big breakthrough. My company, Northern Minerals, owns patents on wollastonite, and the Willsboro mine is operated now by the Interpace Corporation of New Jersey. Our Lewis mine will be used for research until there is a greater demand for the mineral. Most of

what is mined now goes into paints, ceramics, and plastics. Interpace employs only eighty people, but if all I hope for comes true we could hire thousands someday. This weird little mineral could solve all the economic problems in the county, and in a couple of other counties besides."

Burnham inherited a five-thousand-acre estate, Highlands Forge, from his father, and he maintains it with passionate dedication. It borders on Lake Champlain near Willsboro and includes its own small lake, several mountains, guest cottages, a deer park, a geological laboratory, and a cedar-fence-post factory. In addition, it affords one of the most awesome views in the North Country. The squire of all this is fond of showing visitors the estate by Jeep, with a running commentary designed to flatten the rutted dirt roads. "Highlands Forge used to be just that—an old forge town, complete with school and post office," he said during a ride on his property one day. "It went bust, just like the others. I still dig up the damnedest iron tools from time to time, and I've got practically a museum of them back at the main house. Now, over there is the cedar-post factory. We're fortunate in having two men who are experts at hand-stripping cedar. It was almost a forgotten craft until I found these fellows and trained them. I have three other men cutting cedar trees on my property. We Essex men are amazing people, if I do say so myself. One of my old woodsmen—he could pound nails in with his fist. He was totally illiterate, and yet he could memorize complicated mechani-

cal plans and repair just about anything I gave him. Incredible fellow. He raised nine children and always managed by his wits and his self-reliance. You hear a lot about how the North Country man is turning into a welfare bum. Well, if wollastonite becomes really big up here, I haven't the slightest doubt that our men can rise to the occasion and the technological challenge. There's still wealth in these mountains and strength in the people. But we could use a little luck, too."

TITANIUM, wollastonite, bird's-foot trefoil, and the remaining cuttable trees aside, the present-day natural resource of most significant value in the county is the business of tourism and recreation. "Tourism is our meat and potatoes," said a man in county government not long ago. "It brings in the sales tax and profit to our stores. But to be honest, I wish to hell we had some other meat and potatoes. The visitors' money maybe keeps us going from year to year, and I'll say thank God for that. But it's no solution to the perpetual job bind and, besides, it's a lousy way to make a living." Statistics seem to back up this sentiment. The growth rate of personal income in New York State for 1967 was greater than the nation's, but Essex County had the second-lowest share of all the

state's sixty-two counties. Per capita income rose only seventy-eight dollars during that bountiful year. Sullivan County, in the Catskills, which is also kept alive by tourism, had the lowest gain, forty-one dollars. Both gains are well below the national average.

"The Business," as it is sometimes called by those in it, takes on several forms, all closely tied to each other. First and foremost is the one-hundred-and-fifty-year-old resort commerce, made possible by the county's physical features and healthful reputation. While the grand-hotel variation of this has pretty much disappeared, the summer-place-in-the-mountains version is growing in inverse proportion to the availability of rural real estate within a day's drive of the big eastern cities. Well-designed colonies of modest summer and/or winter houses have sprung up throughout the area, bringing seasonal spasms of prosperity to local builders and tradesmen.

But in numbers of tourists and volume of dollars, the "Adirondack Attractions" are the heart of the Business. From May to October, these tourist traps—some manufactured, some natural, some historical, some recreational, and some a little of all four—transform the county into bumper-sticker country, as thousands of middle-class American and Canadian vacationers arrive to take in the sights with their children and pets. The man-made attractions owe their existence to the old-fashioned amusement park and Walt Disney. With such names as Frontier Town ("Ride Shotgun on Stage, Join the Cavalry, Guard

the Fort, Thrill to Wild Rodeos, Travel by Steam Train, See the Pony Express, Help Capture Outlaws, Pow-wow with Indians"), or Santa's Workshop at North Pole, N. Y. ("See his sleigh-bed . . . Feed his many animals . . . Ride the world-wide Christmas Reindeer Carousel and the Candy-Cane Express steam train with a spectacular view . . . You'll watch Santa's Craftsmen at work . . . Surprise your friends with gifts and cards bearing the unique North Pole post mark . . . Talk to Elmer the Elf and Tannenbaum, the talking Christmas tree . . . The First Christmas, the Nativity, is reenacted many times each day—as Santa Claus tells the story and teaches the lesson of Christmas. You will enjoy the live reenactment and reacquaint yourself with the true spirit of Christmas so often overlooked or forgotten in our busy world"), or the Land of Makebelieve ("A funderful world of surprise where painstaking craftsmen have fashioned a place colorful, clean and pint sized"), or the Sterling Alaska Fur and Game Farm ("Home of 1000 Animals . . . Here you will see Animals from Steaming Jungles, Desert Sands, Arctic Wastes"), the emphasis of these attractions is obviously on children, and the travelling middle class has lots of children. Natural attractions such as Ausable Chasm and the summit road to Whiteface Mountain and the historical sites such as Fort Ticonderoga and Crown Point also draw the kiddies. However, the recreation, or sports, part of the Business lures an older, richer crowd, and in the Whiteface–Lake Placid area it has breathed some life into the traditionally dead winter economy.

Skiing, skating, snowmobiling, and even bobsledding are so popular, in fact, that on good weekends the winter-recreation tourists may outnumber the summer, spring, and fall bathers, hikers, campers, fishermen, and hunters combined.

The remaining part of the tourism economy concerns the satellite rings of motels, gas stations, hot-dog stands, laundromats, gift shops, and the like that surround each piece of the Business. These enterprises employ a large segment of the county's working people, but this employment is by and large temporary. Indeed, it is the ephemeral employment inherent in tourism that causes county leaders to view the growth of the Business with something less than joy. For instance, four hundred and eighteen tourism-connected services were listed for Essex County in the 1967 *New York State Statistical Yearbook,* but in the off-season week of March 12th only six hundred and thirty-seven persons were employed by all these services.

The capricious nature of both the elements and the tourists themselves is another reason why some natives nip at the hand that feeds them. The entire economy of the Business, and thus of the region, can be critically hurt by, say, a long January thaw, a rainy Fourth of July, or a snowless Christmas. Essex is probably the only county in New York State where this is true. And nobody really knows just how many tourists may decide in a given summer to visit the seashore instead of the mountains. The Business is iffy at best.

A man who has lived with his predicament for years is Arto Monaco, the creator, owner, and manager of the Land of Makebelieve in Upper Jay, by far the most original of the man-made Adirondack Attractions, or "theme parks," as Monaco calls them. The son of an Italian immigrant father and an Essex County mother, Monaco was raised in the tiny community of Upper Jay, where his father ran a store. He showed an early facility for drawing and painting ("I was too stupid to be anything but an artist") and in 1934 he received some encouragement from the late painter Rockwell Kent, who had just bought a dairy farm in nearby Au Sable Forks. He struck out for Hollywood in 1937, where he began a long career as a cartoonist and set designer for M.G.M. and Warner Brothers. Then, in the Army during World War II, the first idea for a theme park came to him when he was assigned the task of building street-fighting "villages" for training aids ("I won the eighth Legion of Merit ever given for that, before General Eisenhower even got his"). After the war he decided that he was "just a country boy at heart" and returned to Upper Jay where he started a toy factory. "I tried to make really fine hand-crafted circus wagons and trains and that kind of toy," said the trim, mustached Monaco, who favors western-style clothes. "But there wasn't much of a market for quality, although I still get requests from some people who remember those toys as kids and want them for their own children. Designing a theme park was the real bug in my head." Finally, in 1948, he was asked to draw up plans for

the first theme park in the United States—Santa's Workshop at North Pole, N. Y., his present competition about five miles north of Upper Jay, in the town of Wilmington.

"The theme-park idea caught on big," Monaco continued, "and suddenly I was asked to do them all over the Adirondacks. But then what I really wanted most was a park of my own, with a western village and rides on trains and stern-wheelers and old cars and fire engines and an enchanted castle—all scaled down to a kid's size so he feels at ease there. In 1954 I got my financing. It took years of back-breaking work—we build practically everything ourselves here at the Land of Makebelieve—but now I'm finally making a go of it. We've had some bad years, real bad. Even when things are looking up, like during the Montreal Expo in 1967 and '68, the government makes it tough for us. I employ about sixty-five people from May to October, both old and young alike. The summer-job kids I hire to run the rides and things, I have to pay them the minimum wage—a dollar-eighty-five an hour—so I can't afford to pay my older, steadier employees what they're really worth. It costs me eight hundred dollars just to open my doors in the morning. If the weather is rotten, I'm out eight hundred bucks that day.

"I can understand why some people are afraid of tourism up here; they don't want the towns becoming like Lake George, with all that neon and rowdiness. But what they don't understand is that tourism is the one really surviving industry in Essex County. If I go broke, there

are sixty-five people out of work, and no place for them to get new jobs. It's true they go on unemployment anyway from October to May—you should see the caravans of cars going to Saranac Lake to pick up the unemployment checks—but even so, some money you actually earn is better than nothing or constant handouts. There's a lot of talk about light industry saving the day with good-paying, regular jobs. Well, where is it? It's mostly talk. I tried light industry once with my toy factory. It didn't work. Meanwhile, we all got to eat."

There is an old adage woefully repeated by North Country people in the Business: "You make it in the summer or you don't eat all winter." (The reverse is presumably an old adage in Florida.) The ancient saw is still basically true for Essex County, but since the completion of the Northway and with the growing popularity of winter sports, it shows more signs of age all the time, particularly in the Whiteface–Lake Placid area. The little village of Wilmington along the banks of the Ausable River's trout-famous West Branch has benefited from this turn of events almost as much as Lake Placid itself. Over the past ten years it has been transformed into a swirl of motels and restaurants, ranging from the coral-pink hideous to the A-frame functional. An aesthetically in-between example is located near the road to Whiteface Mountain and Lake Placid and the Santa's Workshop theme park. The motel was bought a few years ago by a married couple from Long Island—for some reason, many Wilmington

motels are owned by refugees from Long Island but are staffed by locals—and the emigrés are comparatively happy with their new life. The husband has always liked to cook and so he runs the restaurant, while his wife minds the registration desk in the motel's office. She wears an unmistakable city face that sets her apart from the majority of local ladies; however, her Long Island locutions are slowly giving way to Essex County. "What a weekend!" she said on a Tuesday afternoon following Labor Day. "Jammed almost every night. But that's the way it's been through most of the summer, so I shouldn't complain. From today on, we'll charge half rates, twenty dollars a couple, and we'll be just about half filled, what with the fall-foliage watchers and the hunters. But half filled is a hundred per cent better than nothing. Then, if there's good snow at Whiteface, we'll be full up every winter weekend. The skiing crowd is a little more boisterous than the others, but they're nice folks, usually. To tell you the truth, we'd have a hard time without them, it costs so much to heat this place all winter and the taxes being so high. The spring, that's the worst time for us. Motelwise, we don't do well at all. Canadians come down for the weekends, maybe, and we get some run-off from the Santa's Workshop visitors and some trout fishermen, but so much depends on the weather. It's like dancing on eggshells with the weather. July Fourth weekend was cold as all get-out and I could see the tourists pulling up, jumping out of their cars, and then jumping back in again. It warmed up, though, and some stayed on for a day or two. But we got a bad scare."

As she spoke, three middle-aged women, who looked like school teachers having a last fling before the academic year began, entered the office and inquired about rooms. They wanted one unit with three single beds. The proprietress offered them connecting double rooms for twenty dollars, plus tax. They hesitated, asked if there was TV in both rooms, and, after whispering among themselves, they finally registered. When the proprietress returned from seeing the new guests to their rooms, she said, "We get a lot of them after Labor Day. They come to see the foliage, which is early this year. They're nice, quiet people and some are repeats. No trouble. Very few kids and pets. We didn't see too many like that before they finished the Northway. It's so easy to drive up now from New York or Boston or even Ohio. It's a crying shame that New York State doesn't help us out by advertising more. They push their own public campsites but not us motel owners. We have to contact ski clubs and groups on our own. Whole ski clubs take over the place when the snow is good, but we have to arrange the publicity ourselves."

She smoothed her frosted hair and continued, "I guess I still miss the big shopping centers and the convenience of the city, but, all in all, I like the life up here and the people. We have twelve on our payroll in the busy season, just three or four in the off seasons. We start them at the minimum wage, and when things go well they get bonuses. The folks around here, they understand why we have to let them go when we're not filled. To tell you the truth, I think they actually like the unemployment-insur-

ance deal after working for just twenty weeks. It gives them plenty of time to hunt and fish and so on. If it wasn't for us, they'd probably starve."

A short way up the Whiteface Mountain Memorial Highway is Santa's Workshop at North Pole, N. Y., and Charles Call. Call is said to be a descendant of the legendary Lewis Giant, Joe Call, and he looks every bit of it. His rugged, upcountry appearance is enhanced by a long black beard, which he wears for professional reasons: he acts the role of Joseph in the Nativity Play at Santa's Workshop. "I'm in costume and on stage three times a day when we're open," Call said during the break one afternoon. "A tape recording tells the story of the Nativity, so none of us actors have any lines to speak. The whole thing takes only thirteen minutes. There are nine in the cast in the busy season, but when the tourists thin out, we double up and the shepherds become wise men. Some college kids join us in the summer, but the Virgin Mary, like me, is a local. I've been doing this since 1959 and I like it fine. I used to run a full-time snack bar in Wilmington but it was hard going. I got eight children and I suffer from this asthma, so I really can't work too much. That's why being Joseph here from May to October and then going on unemployment isn't so bad for me. I can get by and I have all that time for my hunting and fishing."

The village of Lake Placid is the closest thing Essex County has to the big time, a place where city ways and a city point of view are not alien. It is a small city in it-

self, filled with such unlikely enterprises as good foreign restaurants, famous department-store branches, expensive jewelry shops, and even a topless à go-go night club. The narrow main street of the village is often as difficult to navigate by car as Madison Avenue on a rainy Tuesday afternoon. In the summer, visitors are actually turned away for lack of vacancies. A world-wide reputation for tourism and recreation is the reason for all this commerce, and the citizens of Lake Placid have long made their peace with the Business.

While the roots of tourism in the village go back well into the nineteenth century, it wasn't until the 1890's that Lake Placid struck it rich. A bookish man with severe hay fever named Melville Louis Kossuth Dewey was responsible. As a compulsive time-saver and priggish intellectual, he was driven to invent the Dewey Decimal Classification System for libraries while still an Amherst undergraduate. In his quest for even greater time-saving methods, he became a leader of the simplified English spelling movement (changing his own first name to "Melvil"), and, later, as librarian of the State of New York, he ran into harsh controversy over his rigid, unorthodox ideas. To assuage his feelings and his hay fever, he bought some land along Mirror Lake (the village of Lake Placid is situated on Mirror Lake, not on Lake Placid) and founded the exclusive Lake Placid Club, where he envisioned the nation's best-bred individuals exchanging interesting ideas in a congenial and healthful setting. Dewey did not allow smoking or drinking in his club, he pushed winter sports mercilessly, and he printed his menus in simplified spell-

ing; still, the place miraculously prospered and it was considered a singular social coup to be invited there, let alone be asked to join. Many of the very rich bought land nearby and built their own estates, using the club as a social center. The club's admission policies also brought it quite a bit of notoriety. A page in the club's 1914 handbook read:

> No one is admitted to full membership til he has been long enuf at the club as associate or gest to know that he sympathizes with its aims and methods. No one wil be receivd as member or gest agenst whom there is any reasonabl physical, moral, social or race objection, or who would be unwelcome to even a small minority. This excludes absoluteli all consumptivs or others whose presence might endanjer helth or modify freedom or enjoyment. Membership rules gives details.
>
> While the club is not open to the public, it welcomes introductions of those likeli to add to its attractions. Stranjers wishing introductions should refer to prominent citizens recognized as leaders of higher interests in their communities, who are likeli either to be members or well known to club members.
>
> Simplifyd speling uzed

A sign supposedly posted near the club's golf course put it more succinctly: NO DOGS, TUBERCULARS, OR JEWS.

(Dewey, it must be said, was not alone in his discriminatory policies. It was common then for other Adirondack hotels to advertise such warnings as "Hebrews will knock vainly for admission.")

At any rate, Dewey and hiz club put Lake Placid on the map and launched winter sports as a desirable alternative to going south for the winter. A New York Central spur line brought trains full of pink-cheeked tourists to Lake Placid all year round, and the flourishing townspeople chose to ignore the sporadic criticism leveled at the club and its pristine surroundings. When Dewey died during the Depression, the club and the village began to die also. The Second World War revived it, when the Army turned the club into a rest and recuperation center, and since then the rambling, brown-shingled buildings have gone through a social and fiscal renaissance. Unrestricted conventions are now avidly sought (at a recent Rotary International Convention held there, which coincided with Passover, the club provided amazed Jewish delegates with matzoth); liquor is served; smoking is permitted; and menus are printed in unsimplified English. However, the private-club part of the complex on Mirror Lake is still very much private. A Jewish resident of the area once remarked, "My liberal friends who are members prefer not to invite me to the club for a drink because they say I'd feel uncomfortable. Maybe I would, maybe I wouldn't, but the truth is I really don't give a damn any more." Today, many of the hotels and motels in Lake Placid have primarily Jewish guests and their ad-

vertisements appear in the *Times* and *Post* alongside the Grossinger's and Concord announcements of learn-to-ski specials and singles weekends. No one, least of all the Lake Placid Chamber of Commerce, seems to mind.

Alan H. Eggleston, the former executive secretary and moving force of the Chamber of Commerce, would look ridiculously out of place anywhere in Essex County but in Lake Placid. His baggy eyes, well-barbered face, and intense manner mark him as an urban operative, the sort of fellow who might be a successful politician's press secretary. But his big-time energies have borne fruit. "The C of C started in the Thirties where Dewey left off," Eggleston told a visitor when he still occupied his office in the newly enlarged Olympic Arena building. "Now, I believe Lake Placid is synonymous with any of the great resorts to the outside world. We're steadily growing here, not really booming, but steadily growing. I once figured out that within seven travelling hours of us eighty million people can reach Lake Placid. Let's hope they don't all decide to come at once, but it gives you an idea of what potential tourism can do for a chronically depressed area."

Eggleston stretched out the fingers of his right hand and held up another finger from his left hand. "There are six ways the money comes in," he went on, "what I call 'access to dollars.' The first is one of the fastest growing—the convention business. A lot of people around here had to change their ideas about diversified conventions in order to survive economically. This is potentially the

most profitable part of the Business. Then, two, there's the tourist on vacation. Some people complain they're stop-and-go types. They still bring in the cash, if not to the better shops. Then there's the sports participant—the skiers, skaters, and what-nots. More every year. Let's see now—number four—there's the sports fan, the guy who comes to watch our hockey games, ski jumps, bobsled races, luge championships, speed skating, and we've even got a bridge tournament scheduled. We've been holding the John F. Kennedy Winter Memorial Games here, with every event from figure skating to snowmobiling. Five, we also get an educational dollar from the private schools nearby, like the North Country School—a private co-ed grammar school—and our own ice-skating school, with professional teachers. Then, lastly, there's the hospital dollar from the new Uihlein Mercy Center, with about two hundred employees, and the W. Alton Jones Science Cell Center, with some sixty people. Some day, we hope to have a whole research and pharmaceutical industry up here and in Saranac Lake. Who can tell?"

Eggleston's mouth drooped with a sudden unpleasant memory. "Oh, we've had our rough setbacks, too," he said. "Ever since we held the Winter Olympics here in 1932, we've been trying to get it back again. We thought we had a chance as the 1968 site, and we moved fast and big. As soon as the 1964 Innsbruck winter games were over, the International Olympic Committee held a meeting to pick the 1968 site. The citizens of Lake Placid kicked in fifty thousand dollars and New York State put

up another thirty thousand, and we sent five teams of two men each to Innsbruck, myself included, to sell the voting delegations on this place. Even with our terrific displays and pitches, we were beaten on the first ballot. The final fight was between Banff and Grenoble, and, of course, Grenoble won out. There's politics involved; De Gaulle recognized Red China before the voting and that made a big impression on some of the leftist delegations. It's more work and heartbreak than fun, those Olympic selling junkets, but we'll probably keep trying for dear old Lake Placid. Naturally, a lot of local merchants were a little irate that we spent so much dough and didn't bring home the bacon. We've learned to make our *own* business now, like the conventions, bobsled championships, parachute-jumping competition, professional archery, which tide us over the lean months.

"Other problems are popping up as we get bigger. Some hippies have discovered the glories of the area and during the summer the transient help has been known to stir up trouble. Also, Lake Placid is surrounded by state land, which makes it damn hard to think about expansion. We're hemmed in here by the state. Growth and expansion in tourism is what will save the North Country, but try to sell that to the Adirondack Forest Preserve fans. I'll tell you one thing—we're not forever-wilders in Lake Placid."

THE opportunities for decent-wage, full-time employment in what remains of Essex County heavy industry are crumpling like the Iroquois braves before Champlain's harquebus. In the spring of 1971, the J. & J. Rogers Company paper mill in Au Sable Forks closed down because of a combination of poor business and a new law calling for an end to the industrial pollution of state waterways. When paper was being made, the swift, rocky Ausable River used to change color from week to week downstream of the mill, depending on what kind of dye the factory was using. Plant life for several miles on the river's run to Lake Champlain was just about nonexistent, and while there were still fish swimming about in the sometimes-green, sometimes-pink murk, they were considered inedible. An efficient waste-disposal system for

the mill and the town would have cost about one and a half million dollars, sixty per cent of which would have been paid by the state and federal governments. However, neither the mill nor the town of Jay (which governs Au Sable Forks) could afford to pay the hefty balance. "The town budget has such a road and welfare drain, I don't see how we could foot the bill," an Au Sable elder explained. "It's kind of funny, though. The six hundred thousand we needed to save the mill and the town, that's just a few bombs and rockets they're dropping on the jungle there in Vietnam every day. Christ, if the government just gave us that money, they could keep a whole American town alive, instead of blowing up a bunch of rubber trees."

The International Paper Company in Ticonderoga has already solved its water-pollution problems, although its past fouling of Lake Champlain with wastes and sludge has prompted an interstate investigation of the matter. In time for the 1971 deadline, the company opened a new pulp-and-paper plant four miles north of the town, and the modern plant meets all state standards for treatment of wastes. The new complex costs seventy-six million dollars and is the lat word in automation. No drastic lay-offs of the one thousand International Paper Company workers are planned, but the chances are slim for an employment boom in Ticonderoga.

So the last hope for economic stability in Essex County rests with that famous, elusive dream of contemporary rural America—light, "clean" industry. But, as the entire

population seems to shout daily, "Where is it?" Every person who asks that question tends to supply a different answer, and every answer has some claim on the truth. Karl Hofmann, the executive director of the Eastern Adirondack Economic Development Commission, feels that one solution lies with training the local youth in a vocational-trades center for the new technological society. He assumes that industry would want to come to a region with a pool of skilled workers. He believes that cheaper, more efficient transportation facilities—perhaps utilizing Lake Champlain as it was used by the Indians and the pioneers—would also help create interest in the area. "We've got literally mountains of mine tailings in Mineville and Tahawus," he said. "It's great material for making cinder blocks and road fill. They used quite a bit of it in the Northway construction. The trouble is, it costs so much to ship out that heavy stuff from up here in the Sticks that it's not economically practical. The upshot is, we don't have a thriving cinder-block industry—and we should."

Arthur Douglas, who is the Democratic County Chairman and the first Democratic town supervisor in the long history of Jay, still hopes political action might be the key to the county's problems. He was a close friend of the late Senator Robert F. Kennedy, and he gained through that friendship some high-level interest in his town's difficulties. "I also worked through Franklin D. Roosevelt, Jr., and Howard Samuels and other politicians I know to get some light industry here," Douglas told a visitor. "They

promised they'd send experts up, at least to advise us about on-the-job training. Some people did show up, but nothing much happened. Now they're all out, and Nixon's in, and I don't know what can be done. Maybe Senator Javits will help."

One rather bitter businessman blamed the natives themselves for discouraging light industry. "Some people around these parts are just plain lazy no-goods," he said. "They give a bad image. They're backward, they're heavy drinkers, and most of them would rather hunt than work. They won't do anything to help themselves—won't tie their own shoelaces unless you pay them for it. By now they're used to living on welfare and from hand to mouth; their kids imitate them and think that's the way life is. Why, hell, you see three generations of one family on welfare sometimes. No self-respect left. Just like with your city colored. Same damn thing. Any unskilled loafer from here could go down to Schenectady and get employment training for free, but how many take advantage of this? I'll tell you: practically no one. And I'll tell you something else: a lot of the unskilled got spoiled years back working for four dollars an hour building the Northway and some government missile sites near Au Sable. What a god-awful waste that was! They abandoned those missile bases almost as soon as they were finished, and they ruined the wage scale for us businessmen. These mountain people get spoiled easy."

Richard W. Lawrence, Jr., of Elizabethtown, who was recently appointed Chairman of the Adirondack Park

Agency, took an opposite view, citing the inborn rugged character of North Country men as a deterrent to change. "People are isolated up here, and they like it that way," Lawrence said. "Most of them feel they can take care of themselves somehow—you can always shoot a deer, or whatever, if you're starving—and they fight the idea of banding together for the greater good of the community. It's a kind of I'm-not-my-brother's-keeper attitude. They fight education and new concepts. They'll have to let their hair down a little. Look what was accomplished just across the lake in Vermont with some good public relations and the cooperation of the people. Executives want to settle in Vermont nowadays. Of course, I can see small changes in the old attitudes. We've learned to speak to neighbors who live more than a couple of miles away, and even to folks in another county. Essex and Franklin finally got together in 1967 and started the North Country Community College, in Saranac Lake. It's just a two-year college, but it's the only one we have. And, I must admit, our people are becoming half civil with the tourists lately. At least they don't give them wrong directions on purpose. That's something."

With harsh bluntness, another businessman offered still another reason for the lack of new industry. "The truth of the matter is that some of the folks around here don't want industry of any kind moving in, because they're afraid that with it will come more wops and Polacks or even—heaven forbid!—niggers and spiks," he said. "They don't want to upset the ethnic balance of things. They like

it the way it is, depression and all."

In spite of the obstacles, a few men have taken a chance on establishing light industry in the county. Such a pioneer is Walter E. Kenzel, who until his retirement in June, 1971, was the president of the Dipak Manufacturing Company, of Westport, a firm that molds expandable Polystyrene for packaging, flotation buoys, and pallets. "I came to Westport from New York City in 1945 to help start a small contracting company," Kenzel told a visitor to his office, an unpretentious storefront near the Dipak plant. "We were doing poorly in the winters, so in 1959 we decided to start a plastics factory by selling stock to certain people in the area. Sort of a self-help project. We converted a barn near Westport and went ahead. It was rough sledding at first, until we hit on this custom-molded Polystyrene. Now we're moving, and we've got seven full-time employees and a salesman who covers the East for us. The future looks pretty good.

"I think the local boys who work for us are as good as they come. They work hard, and they're diligent. But I'm afraid not many businessmen would want to take a chance on our labor pool, the way they do in Vermont, say. Our men don't have the same heritage for machine work that New Englanders do. Businessmen can't be bothered with too much training of employees. The logistics of industry up here limit sales and growth, especially with bulky stuff. There's no getting away from it—we are isolated, even with the Northway. I'll manufacture my products and ship them out as long as it pays me to do it.

But if I have to ship too far it doesn't pay. The way the transportation situation is now, we can't compete with a plant in New Jersey, for instance."

All the knots and loose ends snarling the economy of Essex County eventually come together in one immense, seemingly hopeless tangle called welfare. The welfare problem is what every resident, comfortable or destitute, must live with every day, and for the essentially conservative, individualistic citizenry, living with it is not easy. The generalities of welfare are staggering. Over half of the 1971 county budget went for social services, and although seventy per cent of the expenditure was reimbursed by state and federal funds, the balance was still a frightening drain on taxpayers. (In New York City, where welfare costs are notorious, only one-quarter of the total nine-billion-dollar budget was assigned to social services.) Twenty-eight hundred people out of the total population of thirty-four thousand six hundred received direct county welfare, not including Medicaid. Six hundred and seventy-nine families received United States Department of Agriculture food stamps. And things are getting worse. A shocking twenty-five per cent of the county's total working force was unemployed as of early 1972. People concerned with welfare distribution make up one of the larger and better-paid working groups on the county and town payrolls (inspiring one worker to say that they are welfare cases themselves). At present, welfare costs have risen to nearly five million dollars a year, and they are likely to

continue rising.

However hard the idea of welfare is to swallow, the people of Essex County have been ingesting it for some time. The first recorded minutes of Elizabethtown town meetings, dating back to the early 1800's, contain such references as "Voted that Edw Newell be allowed three Dollars & 25 cents paid to Giles Philips in sickness," and "Voted that the money that is due for Excise to said town be collected by the Poormasters and Let out to use." By 1823, the minutes include such escalated entries as "Voted that the sum of one hundred and fifty Dollars be raised upon the town for the support of the Poor."

The man responsible for trying to make some sense of the welfare tangle is John Owen, a retired naval officer and currently the Commissioner of the Essex County Department of Social Services. Still every bit the courtly officer in his new position, Owen attacks the problem of welfare with military efficiency and tactical reliance on a competent staff. "I have a good tight ship here," Owen told a friend in his Elizabethtown office. "There are two case supervisors and nine case workers, whose attitude is excellent. They try to help in every way, firmly but charitably. Also, we're one of the few counties left that has welfare officers elected in most of our towns, and they are sort of assistants to the county staff. They administer home relief for people who don't receive county benefits and they give aid in emergency cases. They can make certain recommendations, too. But it's our county staff that handles the really expensive troubles—aid to depen-

dent children, old-age assistance, aid for the blind and disabled, Medicaid, and even a new psychiatric clinic. Aid to dependent children is the most pernicious. There are large families up here, and when the father is out of work or disabled or deserts, we have to supplement the family income to keep the children eating and healthy. We have a fairly high incidence of desertion, chronic drunkenness, downright laziness, and even inbreeding. In the backwoods, I'm told you can still find some fathers and daughters producing offspring. Sometimes the families are already so inbred and large, they don't even know that they're mating with close relatives. And of course, we have many destitute old people living here and too many disabled, because of the rigors of work in the North Country. They *all* gobble up the welfare funds, but we don't get any extra reimbursement from Washington or Albany for being a depressed area. We're, however, bound by law to Washington and Albany for distribution of funds, so there's little room for independent judgment, which is a shame, I think.

"My feeling about welfare is that it's a necessary evil. People up here do need assistance, but the government can be too generous sometimes. Where do they draw the line for the poverty level? One man gets welfare and another fellow just over the line gets nothing. I think those marginal people could help themselves more. Still, I suppose you have to draw the line somewhere. And it's true that welfare is blighting the old Adirondack rugged individualist. I've seen good men come in the office and tell

us that handouts are the last thing they want but they just don't know where else to turn. People down on their luck get desperate. But some folks are still scared to death of welfare. They think they'll have their possessions taken away by the government if they accept any help.

"There's a welfare curse on Essex County, going all the way back to Gilliland's time. Maybe it's the hardship of the climate and the rough work. Like everyone else, I believe that new industry is the only real solution."

The town of Jay doesn't elect a welfare officer, which means that Supervisor Arthur Douglas dispenses the home relief and makes recommendations to the county. But Douglas, who also owns an Au Sable Forks bar and grill which is a kind of town parliament, treats the problem in a novel, if not particularly legal, way. "When I was first elected as supervisor," Douglas told a friend one day while presiding over his parliament, "I started this policy of having our welfare recipients work off their checks for the town. Now I admit it probably won't stand up in court but, damn it, it's a good idea and so far nobody's taken me to court on it. Of course, a lot of folks I put to work say they won't vote for me next time around, and that's too bad when every vote counts heavy in a small town like this. But I don't care. I'm doing what I think is right. We start the welfare fellows working for the minimum wage, and some of them are doing so good they get permanent jobs out of it. Naturally, there's some getting welfare in my town who are just not able to work, and we don't bother them. But on the other hand—well, here's a

for instance: There was this man with a bad back. A doctor examined him and said he couldn't work, so we had another doctor look him over and the second doc said there was nothing seriously wrong with his back. Still, the fellow kept getting his disability payments. We gave him town work to pay off the welfare money, and he admits he's a happier man for it. We're happier, too."

Florence Nichols of Elizabethtown is a transplanted city woman who once worked in the county as a state investigator of handicapped children. "Some years back," Miss Nichols said, "I investigated a case of a very sick child in an upcountry cabin. Well, the child could be saved but she needed immediate treatment at the hospital. You'd think there wouldn't be any question about this, but when I appeared at the cabin door, I was met by the father holding a gun. 'You take my kid,' he told me, 'and I'll shoot. Nobody's going to take my kid away to any hospital.' I finally convinced him to put down the gun, but it took a lot of talking and a lot of courage I didn't think I had. Sometimes, I came across families where everyone could use help—the mother had no teeth, the father was crippled, the children were hungry and undernourished and sick. You had to beat down their North Country pride first and then maybe they'd respond. One boy, I remember, had a correctable speech defect which was just ruining his life. I got the school nurse to speak to the mother who finally convinced the father that an operation would give the boy a normal childhood. That story ended happily, thank goodness.

One of my co-workers was determined to get a bathtub for a household with thirteen kids. At least a bathtub! It took years before the mother was won over. That was actually a rare case of the mother just losing her pride completely, dressing in rags, letting herself go, not caring any more. People here are often made to feel anti-welfare, and the welfare workers are just as often to blame for that because of their attitude toward the unfortunate. Inbreeding, drunkenness, illegitimacy, ignorance—especially ignorance—they're all to blame, too."

They are easily spotted in the Grand Union supermarkets after the monthly welfare checks come in and the Department of Agriculture food stamps are purchased. Buying the family food is a family affair, with the father pushing the metal cart through the aisles, his hunting-capped head bent low because he knows he's doing woman's work; the plump, bland-faced mother, in her forties and looking fifty-five, picking items with scrupulous care from the shelves; the children hanging on the cart, on the mother, on the father, their excitement tempered as if they were in church. At first glance, the cart seems to be loaded solely with house-brand ketchup bottles, dozens of them, but on closer examination one can spy through the red barricade boxes of thick spaghetti, institution-size jars of peanut butter, coffee, lard, bacon ends, frozen pizzas, outrageously long loaves of white bread, last week's doughnuts at half price, some cheap hamburger meat, several half-gallon containers of milk, Coca-Cola, and

quart bottles of Genesee Beer. The mother does some rapid arithmetic in her head and concludes that they have bought enough. The children quietly protest that they didn't get any sweets. The mother gives in and selects a party-pack of mixed jellybeans. The father says nothing and pushes the overloaded cart to the check-out counter. Before the groceries are rung up on the register, the food stamps are submitted and the welfare check is cashed with muted ceremony. Then the supermarket clerk looks over the bottles, cans, and packages as they are lined up on the counter and with a practiced eye estimates that they will total less than the check and stamps. The family stands humbly, as if awaiting a judge's decision. At last, the clerk nods and rings up the items; some cash is handed back to the father; the mother grabs the Green Stamps; cardboard cartons and large paper bags are skillfully packed; and the family joins in wheeling the load by cart to the two-toned, crumpled 1959 Chevrolet sedan in the parking lot. The trunk and back seat are crammed with the precious cargo, and an older child is sent to return the cart to the store, riding it like a scooter up to the door. Milk, beer, bread, and other provisions will be purchased throughout the rest of the month at a smaller general store near home, if the money holds out. They certainly will not starve, but the children are often surprised to learn that there is another way of stocking the family larder.

A recent addition to the roster of such welfare cases is the Watts family, as it will be known here. Dwayne

Watts, now in his fifties, was graduated from an Essex County high school during the Depression and luckily found work as a woodcutter for a local sawmill. Because of poor eyesight, he was deferred from the Second World War draft. He took advantage of the wartime manpower shortage to accept a job as a handyman and caretaker for a modest estate near his home town. That job paid slightly more than two thousand dollars a year in 1941—plus certain fringe benefits, such as a share of the vegetable and maple-sugar harvests—and with this stable income, he took for a wife a high-school classmate named, for these purposes, Lucille. They rented a small but neat frame house near the estate and furnished it with whatever they could scrounge from friends, relatives, and Dwayne's employer. In 1951, when Dwayne's yearly salary was raised to $3,120, they felt secure enough to have a child—a boy—and buy a Maytag washing machine on the installment plan. A daughter followed soon after and Dwayne bought outright for cash a postwar Ford owned by a relative. With two growing children and their few modern conveniences, the Watts found it difficult to make ends meet. The electricity and gas bills often went unpaid; parts for the car were obtained from a junkyard. Even the usual party-line telephone was out of the question. Dwayne asked his employer for another raise and was offered an extra two hundred dollars a year, which he accepted. To help out, Lucille worked when she could as a cleaning woman, sometimes bringing her children to the job with her. She was paid seventy-five cents an hour.

Dwayne began to suffer from what he termed "arthuritis," a malady common to North Country people, old and young. His knees, ankles, and hands swelled badly and gave him severe pain, particularly in the winter. He declined to see a doctor because of the cost (he and Lucille boasted that they hadn't been to a doctor more than six times, including the births of their children, until 1968). The pain and swelling grew worse. In 1962, after twenty-one years of work for the estate, Dwayne asked his employer for yet another raise to meet his bills. This time, he was offered what amounted to the equivalent of the state minimum wage. Dwayne quit his job in disgust. He spent most of his time thereafter sulking at home and nursing his ailment with aspirin and rye whiskey, while Lucille did more domestic work. There were few jobs available for unskilled labor, especially chronically sick unskilled labor, but Dwayne had enough pride left to make work for himself. In the late summer, he asked and received permission to gather pine cones on private woodlands, which he then took to a seedling plant in huge burlap sacks. The plant would accept only the perfect cones—to be boiled open for the seeds and then dried and painted for Christmas decorations—and Dwayne was paid fifteen dollars for a full sack of acceptable cones. It usually took him two days of foraging through the woods on his hands and knees to fill one sack with cones that the squirrels hadn't damaged first. He supplemented the family diet with whatever edible animal he could shoot or trap, and he let it be known that he was available for odd

jobs around the village. The odd jobs rarely materialized. He wanted to do some woodcutting on the Northway construction, but he heard that a woodcutter had to bring his own portable power saw and Dwayne couldn't afford to buy a power saw. The one thing he absolutely rejected was to go on any sort of welfare.

Dwayne's health deteriorated; it was so bad that on certain mornings he was unable to get out of bed. He steadfastly refused to consult a doctor, even though his wife and friends assured him that a doctor wouldn't demand payment right away. "He was always a stubborn man," Lucille said recently, "real North Country stubborn. When that Medicaid performance came in, I told him we ought to apply for it and he could get seen to. But then somebody in the village told Dwayne that the state would come and take away his car and what-have-you if he applied, so we didn't do nothing. Then, one day in 1967, he collapsed and went into a faint, and we had to take him to the hospital. It turned out it wasn't just arthuritis that was bothering him all along but a kind of blood-circulation trouble, and now his heart's on the blink besides. His eyesight's going, too. We finally had to get Medicaid—they didn't take nothing away from us—and since the beginning of 1968, we're on county welfare, the old surplus food hand out, and now the government food stamps. There still isn't enough money for the rent and everything else. The boy quit school and he's in the Youth Corps now—he almost made the price of a car for himself—and pretty soon he'll go in the Army, I guess.

The girl is in school, thank the Lord, and I figure she'll do all right, being pretty and all. I can't work at cleaning so much nowadays because of taking care of Dwayne, when he's not in the hospital. He lies in bed talking to himself, swearing and everything, half out of his mind. The doctors say he may never get any better. I don't know, I'm at the end of my rope. Seems like nothing has gone right with us lately. I guess we made a mistake in not getting Dwayne seen to sooner, but we worried about the bills so. Never could get even. I don't know why. We always were willing to work—Dwayne's no loafer, I can tell you that—but we just couldn't make do with the money he was paid. The welfare and the Medicaid are good things, I figure. They just about saved our lives. But it hurts to take them. There's nothing else we can do."

A natural consequence of an urban depressed and welfare-supported area is usually a marked increase in the crime rate, especially in crimes of violence. This is not true of the North Country, where the sparsity of the population encourages introspective brooding rather than open fury against society. Just as the population of Essex County has remained fairly static over the past several decades, so has the number of prisoners admitted to the county jail, and very few of those prisoners have been arrested for anything more serious than drunken driving. For example, only two murders worthy of the name have been committed in the county since 1882; both of them, as county partisans like to point out, were the work of

"outsiders."

The first involved an extraordinary Portuguese named Harry Delecnae Debosny, who spoke six languages, was educated in Paris, took part in polar expeditions and the Crimean War, and somehow, in 1882, found his way to the hamlet of Essex, where he married Elizabeth Wells. Two months after the nuptials, he invited his wife to a picnic lunch in the woods near Westport. Apparently, because she wouldn't hand over three hundred dollars he knew she was hiding from him, he cut her throat and covered her body with leaves and sticks. A neighbor saw Debosny slink from the woods alone, and, with the innate suspicion any decent North Country man has for outsiders, he investigated, finding the untouched lunch and a lot of gore. A posse was summoned and Debosny was captured at the Essex dock, while waiting for a Lake Champlain steamboat to Canada. He was asked for his coat, from which two pistols were confiscated before it was given back to him. "It's no good to me now," said Debosny. Five days later, he was tried, convicted of murder, and was sentenced "to hang by his neck until dead, dead, dead." Awaiting this execution in triplicate, Debosny sold his body to a doctor for fifteen dollars, with which he bought a suit to be hanged in. He willed his eyes to another doctor, at no cost, for research. At one point, he desperately tried to kill himself by hitting his head against the cell wall. Finally, in April of the following year, he was hanged by the sheriff. The noose, hanging weight, and manacles are on permanent display in

the Adirondack Center Museum in Elizabethtown.

The other murder case turned into one of the biggest and costliest manhunts in New York State history. A deserter from a Louisiana Air Force base, who had served for many years as a navigator–bombardier under the alias Major James Arlon Call, turned up in Lake Placid during the summer of 1954. He was caught in the act of burglarizing a vacant summer home by three village policemen who were on a special alert because of a jewelry theft at the Lake Placid Club a few days before. Call killed one officer with his pistol and wounded the other two, and then fled into the wilderness. As many as five hundred and fifty state troopers and volunteers surrounded and searched the Adirondack bush for a 104 days, trying to flush him out. Several volunteers were nearly shot by other volunteers, which must have amused Call who expertly utilized his Air Force survival training to escape through the mountains to New York City. He took a bus west and was apprehended for robbery in Reno three months later, and he might have gotten off with a light Nevada sentence if a reporter hadn't spotted a newspaper clipping of the Lake Placid murder among his belongings.

"Vanity did Major Call in," said Kenneth E. Goodspeed, a retired state trooper who had served on the fruitless Call roadblocks and is now the Essex County sheriff. "That's the way it is with most of the bad ones. Fortunately, we don't have many bad folks around here." Sheriff Goodspeed is every American county's ideal of what a strong, honest cop should look like, with his brush-cut sil-

ver hair, penetrating blue eyes, and stern chin. He spends most of his time in the sheriff's office at the three-story county jail, one of a complex of county-governmental buildings in Elizabethtown. (The county provides the sheriff and his wife with a red-brick house adjacent to the jail.) Born in the Bronx, Goodspeed joined the State Police in his early twenties and was assigned to Essex County, where he has been ever since. He retired from the troopers in 1961, and in 1966 he was elected sheriff. As a rookie trooper, he was given the task of grooming the horses the State Police once used to patrol the North Country. "When the horses were finally retired and we all got cars," Goodspeed said, "I was in on one of the last rumrunner chases in these parts. It was just the reverse of the old Prohibition chases, though—we were after local distillers running their raw alcohol up to Canada, where there was a good market for the cheap stuff. I never caught the man because our captain put governors on the cars."

The State Police still receive ninety-five per cent of the calls for aid in the county, the sheriff explained, because they are better equipped and have more personnel than the sheriff's office or the village constabularies. "But we're kept busy," Goodspeed continued, "what with the court work and all the civil and some criminal calls and maintaining maximum security in the county jail. I try to keep a clean, quiet house here, and we haven't had an escape since I've been in office. There are thirteen men on my staff—an under-sheriff, a civil deputy, and the rest are

deputy-sheriff jailers—but we are allowed only one patrol car, a station wagon for transporting prisoners, and a boat for the lakes. We're lucky to have the staff we do; the starting pay for peace officers is terribly low, even after I got it raised to just over fifty-six hundred a year for a forty-hour week. On top of that, I am personally responsible for my deputies' acts and omissions. If something went wrong, I'd have to pay out of my own pocket above what I'm bonded for, since I'm an elected official. But still, I like this job. Essex County is really my home. I forget what the Bronx looks like.

"If we have a law problem up here, it's public intoxication. Most of our prisoners are in for that, with drunken driving running second. Then there are the hitchhiking cases, which the troopers pick up usually on the Northway and deliver to us. They just brought in a colored kid today who was bumming his way to Canada. He'll stay overnight and tomorrow we'll drive him to the county line and see if we can get him a good ride up to Montreal. Kids are more and more of a problem, both the locals and the ones passing through. Speeding, intoxication, drugs, reckless driving, and petty thefts are their troubles, especially in the summer with tourist kids adding to the population. Just like in the city, it seems parents hereabouts aren't interested in where their children are or what they're doing. We're getting a good bit more drug trouble now than we were two years ago. North Country young people aren't the way they were in the old days. They learn too fast from the TV and movies about vio-

lence and so forth. Of course, this being not one of your richer counties, civil repossession is a big headache. People out of work and on welfare still overbuy, since the stores almost never bother to check somebody's credit. Poverty around here, no matter how bad, always seems to have a car, a TV set, a deepfreeze—that is, until the sheriff is called to take them away."

No issue connected with crime is as hotly felt in Essex County as gun control. A generally reasonably native will deliver a lengthy, harsh dissertation on law and order in the city streets, only to exempt himself from gun-owning restrictions. The rifle is still very much the symbol of the basic pioneer man in the North Country, and it still has basic pioneer uses, providing meat for the table, protection for the family and property, and sport for its owner. Lifelong hunters, like Hubert Burrell, have several firearms and take loving care of them. Burrell, until his heart trouble curtailed his deerstalking, thought of his favorite Savage rifle as an extension of his food budget, and any prohibitive registration fee would upset that budget, if not ruin it. The same is true for most of the other men in the region. At the very least, they use their rifles for target practice or for shooting rats in the town dumps or keeping unwanted animals away from their homes and gardens. Even Supervisor Arthur Douglas, a political liberal and an admirer of the late Robert F. Kennedy, has a sign in his Au Sable Forks bar reading: IF GUNS ARE OUTLAWED ONLY OUTLAWS WILL HAVE GUNS. He is, however, against mail-order gun sales and believes pistol permits

should be harder to obtain, but he feels registration fees would be an impossible burden for men who hunt for food. Few, if any, customers in his bar disagree with him. Sheriff Goodspeed doesn't disagree, either. "We have so little shootings, accidental or otherwise," he said. "Our people learn how to use guns from childhood on—even the girls—so they know about firearms and they respect them. What's more, they need them. There's still plenty of lonely wilderness around. But I'm personally against mail-order gun sales. When a man buys a rifle from somebody up here, his habits and temper are known pretty well. No one is foolish enough to sell a gun to a crazy neighbor, and certainly not to a suspicious stranger. Lucky for me, guns aren't much of a problem."

The Office of the Sheriff and the Department of Social Services are two large functions of an expanding county governmental system. A breakdown of the system shows it to be quite unlike more urban counties. For example, there is no chief executive; the position closest to such an office is Chairman of the Board of Supervisors. The board is a legislative body consisting of the elected heads of the eighteen townships—namely, in order of population, North Elba, Moriah, Ticonderoga, Jay, Chesterfield, Willsboro, Crown Point, Westport, Elizabethtown, St. Armand, Newcomb, Essex, Schroon, Lewis, Keene, Minerva, Wilmington, and North Hudson. The chairman is chosen from among and by the supervisors for a one-year term, and with him rests most of the power in the county, although it is mainly in a legislative sense. By virtue of his

office, he and the Budget Director (another supervisor) can control appropriations and operations for the various executive departments: the offices of County Clerk, Treasurer, Sheriff, Social Services, Auditor, Veterans' Affairs, Civil Service, Fire Co-ordinator, Civil Defense, Coroner, Schools, Mental Health, Highways, Weights and Measures, Elections, Probations, County Nurses, and even the County Historian. Still, their dispositions are subject to votes by the board and its committees.

The judicial branch is headed by the Essex County Judge (who is also Surrogate and Family Court Judge) and includes his two clerks, a district attorney, an assistant district attorney, and a county attorney who acts as a counsel to the Board of Supervisors. A grand jury is readily impanelled when the need arises.

On the town level (communities within townships are "villages," some being incorporated and having mayors and constables), the elected offices vary slightly but the usual hierarchy is: supervisor, town clerk, two town justices of the peace, two councilmen, three assessors, collector, superintendent of highways, and welfare officer. In the case of North Hudson, the paid, elected officers number eleven, or five per cent of the town's total population of two hundred and twenty. Several other North Hudson citizens work for the town in appointive capacities. In such inefficient circumstances, it is not surprising that the government turns out to be the biggest employer in wages paid in the entire county, a situation viewed by the average North Country man with some mixed emotions.

The Board of Supervisors meets on the first Monday of every month in its own room on the top floor of the oldest Elizabethtown county building. (The various committees convene throughout each week, however.) The meeting place resembles a refurbished classroom of an overcrowded elementary school, with light-green, Formica-topped desks jammed into every available bit of space before a plain rostrum. An American flag graces one side of the rostrum and a calendar advertising the Horton Strong Garage in Crown Point completes the decor. The supervisors, most of them large men attired in costumes ranging from business suits to sport shirts and slacks, seem to have no place to put their feet, like overgrown adolescents at a soda fountain. Once they've managed to squeeze behind their desks, they stretch their legs into the aisle and the prevailing tone of folksy decorum is set for the meeting.

On Monday morning, August 5, 1968, the session was called to order from the rostrum by George Haselton, Supervisor of Wilmington and Chairman of the Board. A gentle, soft-spoken Republican, Haselton commanded immediate and friendly respect from his colleagues, only four of whom are Democrats. Zelma A. Cook, the sharp-featured, matronly Clerk of the Board, then called the roll, and, satisfied that all her charges were present, she launched into the business at hand with dispatch. Resolutions dealing with such subjects as extensions of rights-of-way, the pay scale of a newly created part-time job, the rescinding of certain old resolutions were rapidly read by the clerk, then moved, seconded, and either

passed or defeated by voice vote. Finally, one resolution halted the droning routine and inspired some debate. The issue was whether the Elizabethtown Community Hospital, a private institution next door to the county-supported Horace Nye Infirmary, could use the laundry facilities of the infirmary. One supervisor felt that this would deny private enterprise in nearby communities a chance to gain by the hospital's formidable laundry needs, and, besides, he wasn't sure it was legal for a private institution to use, free, the facilities of a public institution. County Attorney Harlan Carson was asked to give his opinion on the legality question; as far as he could see, it was legal. The issue was argued for several more minutes until everybody seemed to sense that he was merely repeating himself. The issue was shelved.

Resolution 165, firmly opposing any contemplated dam across the Hudson River in the vicinity of Newcomb, was carried unanimously and with some emotion. It was pointed out that in the event of such a reservoir project, the Newcomb schoolhouse would be under fifty feet of water, most residential areas would be flooded, and scenic public lands would be ruined. "Why don't the miserable cities get their water by cleaning up the Hudson instead of damming it?" said one red-faced supervisor in an aside.

Sheriff Goodspeed suddenly appeared in the room to plead his case for increasing his liability bond from fifteen thousand to one hundred thousand dollars. He cited the example of a sheriff in another New York county who was

sued for one hundred and fifty thousand dollars because of a deputy's negligence. That sheriff, Goodspeed said sadly, lost the suit and is horrendously in debt as a result. The plea was treated sympathetically by the supervisors and was referred to the proper committee.

Other matters were swiftly dealt with: surplus equipment for Civil Defense ("None available"), the unwanted but necessary merger of Essex and Franklin Counties' federal poverty funds program ("Will the regional office be called Essex–Franklin O.E.O. or Franklin–Essex O.E.O.?"), the legal bargaining agent for county employees ("Can they bargain on county property and on county time?"), highway improvements ("Roads, roads, roads—if it isn't welfare, it's roads!"), and the written request of a Moriah lady to construct a sign directing tourists to the Lake Champlain Bridge ("The poor woman spends her whole day answering the same fool question"). The North Elba supervisor, who was also a successful businessman from Lake Placid, complained about lights being left on in county offices during the noon lunch hour. "We already have a seventeen-hundred-dollar-a-year light bill as it is," he said amid general laughter. As the representative of the most populous town, he has more votes under the board's weighted voting system than most of the other supervisors. The light-burning question was therefore taken under advisement. While the mood was right, another supervisor moved for adjournment. The motion was zestfully seconded and carried, and all present repaired to the Little Tavern down the hill from the historic arsenal

site for drinks, a long lunch, and some good old-fashioned politics talk.

The whole spectrum of American political sentiment was explored over open steak sandwiches and whiskey. Law and order was the most commonly discussed issue and it soon became synonymous with the Negro problem. "Our only Negro problem up here," remarked a smiling supervisor, "is that we don't have a Negro problem."

"That's absolutely true," said another, not smiling. "There's never been any trouble with the few colored we've got, and that includes colored tourists and the colored servicemen from the Plattsburgh Air Force Base. Why, up in the north part of the county, there's a jazz combo including a Negro called Three Cats and a Coon. They're as happy playing together as any three white men. Darn good, too, I understand."

A dour supervisor chimed in, "I don't go for this black-power stuff and all these riots. The city colored have to work for their keep, just like everyone else. If we rioted, what would it get our poor?"

"Maybe it's not such a bad idea," a colleague joked. There was nervous laughter. A luncheon guest suggested that if the city colored have to work for their keep, so should the rural whites. Everyone heartily agreed.

A NORTH COUNTRY chronicler, H. P. Smith, wrote in 1885: "Essex County, fortunately for itself, has never been a political hotbed. While its inhabitants have always felt a deep and abiding interest in public affairs and have shown their political preferences at the polls and supported each his party with earnest deeds, still it has never witnessed the unseemly strifes, the bitter wrangling and the persistent struggle for this or that party success, office or emolument that have characterized some localities. The county is Republican in politics and succeeding the active political campaign of 1860 gave a majority for Lincoln." And, it must be added, for every Republican presidential candidate since, with the notable exception of Barry Goldwater. Registration is better than

two to one Republican, yet in 1964 the voting ratio was reversed in favor of Lyndon Johnson. But with the 1968 elections, the ratio returned to normal, even though George Wallace attracted five per cent of the vote. The citizens of Essex County consistently send Republicans to the New York State Assembly and Senate, and they just as doggedly help reelect Senator Jacob K. Javits and the stodgy Representative of the Thirtieth Congressional District, Carleton J. King.

While most of H. P. Smith's nineteenth century political observation still holds true, it is nevertheless significant that Essex voters take their politics very seriously, especially on the town level. A Democrat, even a liberal Democrat, who campaigns hard and impresses a town can win, as Supervisor Douglas proved in Jay. Although the town's dispersed population is just over two thousand, Douglas put together a strenuous "shoe-leather" campaign in 1965, managed by his son, Thomas. The expenses, all locally donated, were fifteen hundred dollars, most of which went for newspaper ads, candy bars, and cigars. Douglas spent hour after hour discussing issues with as few as two or three voters in barbershops, general stores, farmyards, and his own tavern, and this diligence paid off. He was easily reelected in 1967, 1969, and 1971. (Douglas's victories were made all the sweeter because he won handily in the Republican two-thirds of Au Sable Forks, the town of Jay's most populous village. The other third of Au Sable Forks is across the Ausable River in the Clinton County town of Black Brook and is predomi-

nantly Democratic, due to the influence of urban Plattsburgh. The Jay town government has no authority in the Black Brook third. This capricious geography is also a nagging problem for two other villages in Essex County—Keeseville and Saranac Lake. One-quarter of Keeseville is in Clinton County and three-quarters of Saranac Lake is in Franklin County. "It's like having two Presidents of the United States," said a political leader. "These split-village governments just can't seem to get together for the good of the whole village. Sometimes, they even try to drive each other out of business. Snow plows will stop plowing in the middle of a bridge and tax assessors often try to undercut each other. It can be a hell of a situation.")

It is not surprising to find in this almost monolithic hotbed of Republicanism a small reactionary element, and it is equally unastonishing that the right-wing faction should be located in the Saranac Lake—Lake Placid region, the conservative territory of the late eccentric Melvil(le) Dewey and his Lake Placid Club. The reactionaries have as their official outlet a John Birch Society chapter, to which several professional people, including doctors, belong. (One of the medical members has been known to use a card bearing the rhetorical question: WHY ARE WE LOSING IN VIETNAM? to cover his patients' eyes in optical tests. When an unsettled patient once told this doctor that his Birch Society methods were oddly similar to Communist methods, the doctor asked him to sign a statement admitting that he had called the physician a

Red.) In the twenties and thirties, however, a much stranger group of reactionaries surfaced in the county—the Ku Klux Klan. Since Negroes and Jews were practically nonexistent as year-round residents, the Klan had only Catholics, particularly those of French-Canadian ancestry, to badger. A few crosses were burned and some roadside boulders were painted at night with three white K's, but, fortunately, nothing more serious occurred. Part of the anti-Catholic sentiment was rooted in the establishment of a parochial school that was academically superior to the local public school. Then, as now, the general attitude was to laugh off the extremists as a bunch of oddballs who like to meddle in other people's business.

What is quite surprising to find in Essex County is the thin but continuing presence of left-wing residents. It started, of course, with Gerrit Smith and John Brown and their radical experimentation of the mid-1800's. It burst into the twentieth century with the unlikely appearance in the hamlet of Keene Valley of Maxim Gorky. Maxim the Bitter had taken part in the abortive 1905 Russian Revolution and barely escaped the Tsarist police with his life. Leaving his wife and child behind in Russia, he sailed with his mistress, an actress named Maria Feodorovna Andreyeva, for New York City, where he was greeted as a dashing revolutionary hero by the literati and the press (GORKY IN TEARS AT GRANT'S TOMB, ran one headline). The Russian Embassy was embarrassed by the adulation for this budding Bolshevik and let it be known that Maria Feodorovna and Gorky were living together

in sin at the Hotel Belleclaire. The literati and the press, in one of their more flagrant moral reversals, turned on their idol overnight. Mark Twain refused to have anything to do with Gorky, after warmly meeting with him just a few days before, and the *Sun* screamed editorially, "The purity of our inns is threatened!" The purity of our inns was ultimately preserved, however, when Gorky and his mistress were kicked out of the Belleclaire and hounded into yet another exile to a friend's Adirondack cottage in Keene Valley. They spent the whole summer of 1906 there, experimenting with John Dewey and other sympathetic Americans in an utopian socialistic community. "In the evening," a Gorky biographer wrote, "they would climb trees, and from his perch Gorky would teach them Russian phrases. One of these was: *Lyubitye drug druga*—love one another." Gorky found time during that Adirondack summer to write, with anger and passion, his worst and most revolutionary novel, *Mother,* which became the prototype of all maudlin Soviet "message" literature. The Keene Valley utopian community dissolved with Gorky's departure for Capri and the hot politics of Europe, once the North Country winter set in. It is noteworthy, though, that the hounding of Gorky stopped as soon as he fled to Essex County. In later years, he remembered his summer there as the only pleasant part of his trip to America.

In 1928, another gentleman of a left-wing, artistic persuasion, the late Rockwell Kent, visited the county, fell in love with it, bought a working dairy farm, and stayed on.

His enthusiasm for the stark beauty and isolation of the wilderness attracted others of roughly left-wing political views, among them film director Lewis Milestone, writers Donald Ogden Stewart and Ella Winter, and editors Louis Untermeyer and Angus Cameron. Cameron, like Gorky, was hounded into rural exile, but, in his case, it was the hectoring of the Senate Internal Security Subcommittee in the dark days of the early 1950's. Blacklisted and shunned by most of his associates, Cameron was fully accepted by the North Country people as an individual and an equal, particularly since he loves to hunt and fish. There was some gossip about his frequent trips to Washington, but his neighbors respected his rights to privacy and personal convictions. "It was fantastic," said Cameron, now an editor at Knopf and a resident of Connecticut, "how no one made any trouble for me or my family up there. When you consider the informing, distrustful climate in this country at the time, it's really amazing. A lot of my neighbors were paid visits by the F.B.I., and when they were asked questions about me, they'd say, 'Why don't you just walk over to his house and ask him yourself?' One friend of mine, a big, generous, retired state trooper, no less, used to say, 'I never tell anything on anyone, specially to the F.B.I.' Those people up there are as decent as they come."

Rockwell Kent's tenure as a North Country dairy farmer and resident artist hadn't always been so serene, however. A Marxist and an activist to his Yankee core, Kent was involved in some local political upheavals that

flew in the face of H. P. Smith's observation that the county "has never witnessed the unseemly strifes, the bitter wrangling and the persistent struggle for this or that party success." Foremost among these was what was known as the Jay Revolt of 1933. Kent and some of his fellow Jay farmers found themselves going broke at a faster rate than their other Depression-weary colleagues. One reason was the inequitable tax assessments on outlying farms, as opposed to places of business in villages. These unfair assessments were the work of the "Ring," a cabal of hard-nosed Republican politicians, businessmen, mill executives, and bankers. Although Kent was considered an outsider and a newcomer, he roused the farmers to indignant action and, as it turned out, to arms. They formed the Jay Taxpayers Association, electing Kent chairman, in order to investigate the town's badly inflated finances. One investigation led to another and soon the Jay Taxpayers Association blossomed into the Essex County Taxpayers Association. Graft and misuse of public funds were exposed on such a large scale that Governor Lehman assigned four state examiners to audit the mess. The examiners discovered the fiscal condition of Essex County to be the worst in New York State, with an incredible (for the period) general debt of $1,600,000. One of the items exposed was the expenditure of forty-nine thousand county dollars for the Lake Placid Olympic Arena, to which the taxpayers had no title. (Similar instances of graft have come to light over the past ten years in an investigation of finances in nearby Hamilton

County; politicians in remote rural areas often have fingers as sticky as their urban cousins, sometimes stickier.) But it was on the town level that Kent and his band of rebels stirred up the most trouble. They defied the Ring and most pointedly Fred A. Torrance, the Supervisor of Jay. A reform slate of Republican candidates for town offices was put up by Kent's group and the town was sharply split down the middle. Oral and printed charges flew back and forth: "I hesitate to brand the Kent statements by their true name," wrote Supervisor Torrance in a handbill. "Get the facts and all the facts and do your own branding. You might use a hotter iron than my charitable and unexcitable disposition would suggest." Armed J.T.A. members had to patrol the Kent fences because word got out that "a hotter iron" would indeed be used, specifically against the Kent barn and his prize Jerseys. Intruders were indeed captured and some shots were fired. Just before the elections, the J.T.A. was neatly double-crossed when the Ring made an unholy alliance with the ineffectual Democrats of the town, a coalition that would have been thought next to impossible a few months before. The bipartisan slate edged out Kent's radical Republicans, but election eve was marked by a donnybrook on the Jay Village Green. The State Police were called in to restore order, and although no serious injuries resulted, it took years for the political wounds to heal. There was an immediate improvement in town and county government, however.

In the years before his death on March 13, 1971, Rock-

well Kent was still in the thick of things. Up to his dying day, he had clear, penetrating hazel eyes and a posture that would have been the envy of an infantry captain; he smoked (Kents) incessantly and never drank less than three vicious Martinis a day; and he painted his familiar heroic figures and landscapes with a steady hand. His only concessions to eighty-eight vital years were a Pacemaker and a hearing aid. In April, 1969, a fire started by a freak bolt of lightning in the middle of the night destroyed the charming, cluttered house Kent and his wife, Sally, cherished as a kind of museum of their lives. Set near a copse of towering pines on his three-hundred-acre dairy farm (called Asgaard, from an Icelandic poet's name for a city of the gods), the deceptively small house was filled with Kent's paintings, thousands of books, harpoons and whale bones from his years in Greenland and Newfoundland, and seemingly limitless mementoes of old and new radical crusades. The Au Sable Forks Fire Department managed to save several Kent paintings, and the Kents themselves somehow managed to save their own lives. They lost little time in rebuilding a smaller version the main house, where Sally Kent still lives.

Before the fire, Kent told a visitor to his home about a radical's life in the North Country. "Oh, the Jay Revolt was just one of the scrapes I got into up here," he said, hardly disguising his joy. "I once led a one-man war against the Delaware and Hudson Railroad when they tried to discontinue passenger service on the spur line from Plattsburgh to Au Sable Forks. Now there was a

battle! I had the whole state up in arms. I finally lost, as I usually do, but the railroad knew it was in a fight. Then, in 1942, I invited some Russian students from Columbia University to spend Christmas here at the farm, because I thought it would remind them of home. Sure enough, it did and we all had a wonderful time. Unions contributed to the transportation costs and a few local folks objected, naturally, but that was during the war and Russia was our great ally then. The Russians are a wonderful, happy people, like us when we're at our best.

"The worst mess for me personally was in 1948. I was a big supporter of Henry Wallace and the Progressive Party in the elections, so much so that I ran for Congress from this district on the Progressive ticket. I also had printed on my Asgaard Dairy bottle caps VOTE FOR WALLACE and I sent out newsletters to my regular customers. Well, I didn't do too bad in the elections—though I lost, of course—but I had to suffer through a boycott of my milk. The American Legion was behind that. Pretty soon, two Catholic fellows who were working for me were ordered off the job by their church, and a lot of wild rumors started up, like we were having orgies and spy meetings at Asgaard and what the devil not. It wasn't long before I had to sell my dairy business. But, you know, two can play that boycott game. I still don't buy merchandise at the Au Sable stores. We go all the way to Keeseville for our groceries. I'm kind of funny that way. I refuse to pay the war tax on toll telephone calls, so I do a lot of letter writing—it's nicer, anyway—and I make col-

lect calls. Not very pleasant for my friends, I'm afraid."

The artist–farmer gazed out his window at the huge white cow barn set in sunny fields full of corn, alfalfa, and hay, with the bluish-gray Adirondack peaks making a spectacular solid-wall background. "I've painted and drawn this view I don't know how many times, and it still thrills me," he said. "But I don't get outside so much any more. Years ago, I'd go off on my horse into the hills all day long, exploring the old mine ruins and forests, or I'd putter around the farm. My Mr. Emerson and his sons run the farm now, with all that machinery." (They still do.) "Asgaard was the first modern farm in these parts. The Rockefellers tried to woo away Mr. Emerson to operate their farm in Tarrytown, but he turned them down. He still milks our forty-five Jerseys and we sell the milk to a man who trucks it to Massachusetts. We get a better price in Massachusetts, but even so, we're lucky to break even. You know, most dairy farmers keep Holsteins because of the quantity of milk they produce; it's hard to make money out of my Jerseys, and few folks appreciate the high butterfat content of Jersey milk. Quantity over quality, that's the way it is nowadays.

"I love the North—the colder and farther north the better. Sally and I went to Newfoundland recently as the guests of the Premier—a good Socialist, by the way—because the provincial government wanted to atone for kicking me out during World War I when they thought I was a German spy. Imagine me, a German spy! We had a great time, and I hope medical science can keep me

around long enough so I can go to Greenland again. We were in Russia a couple of years ago, where I was awarded the Lenin Peace Prize. It came to $28,888.88, and I gave ten thousand of it to the women and children of North Vietnam. Well, you can imagine the stink around here over that. Our glorious Congressman Carleton King raised one hell of a fuss, but, still, most of the people here are friendly to me, just so long as we avoid talking politics. The young folks, though, they're terrific today. You can really talk to them about anything. They sometimes come to visit from Plattsburgh State College. I have hope in this new generation, by God."

When the subject of Rockwell Kent comes up in the living rooms and porches of Essex County, he is discussed with grudging respect. Kent was certainly the only Lenin Peace Prize winner in the North Country, and aside from Kate Smith in Lake Placid, he was the only resident celebrity in the county. The word "ornery" is often used to describe him; in local parlance, the word has a meliorative quality. No knowledge of a 1948 boycott against his dairy is ever admitted. A few think the lightning bolt that destroyed his beloved house was an act of God in more ways than one. As for his ten-thousand-dollar donation to the North Vietnamese women and children out of his Lenin Peace Prize money, the prevailing attitude can be summed up by what one Jay townsman said: "I don't give a hoot what Kent does with his money. It's his, isn't it? Why, he can take it up on top of Whiteface and throw it to the wind, for all I care."

Not many of Rockwell Kent's neighbors were overly impressed by the presence of a practicing artist in their midst. Culture, in the compulsive urban sense, is still a big word in Essex County, but unpretentious, homegrown examples of it do exist. In an area so full of history, it would be hard to avoid. Elizabethtown, as the county seat and the center of the establishment, is the cultural hub, with its sedate, timeworn facades, a well-educated upper class, and the Essex County Historical Society which operates the Adirondack Center Museum and Colonial Garden. The museum is housed in an ancient former school building (separate portals are still marked GIRLS and BOYS) and it is a product of local initiative and pride. Attics, cellars, and barns all over the county were searched for pioneer implements and furniture, all of which was cheerfully donated to form the museum's original displays in 1955. Since then, the museum has acquired an original Elizabethtown–Westport stagecoach, striking collections of early costumes and dolls, exhibits of Indian and Adirondack lore, a research library, a room honoring three generations of the judicial Hand family (Elizabethtown's most renowned clan), a display of artifacts loaned by the Crown Point Foundation, and an authentic replica of a colonial garden. It is an informal place; visitors are encouraged to handle things and children may sit in the stagecoach, if they are careful. Very little of value has been stolen through the years. Besides the Adirondack Center and the historical exhibitions at Crown Point, Ticonderoga, and John Brown's Farm,

there are even more humble instances of cultural self-reliance in the county. An abandoned Lake Placid railroad station has been converted into the meager but nevertheless winning Lake Placid–North Elba Museum, and the 1828 Allen Penfield Homestead in remote Ironville offers a superb example of Federal architecture, handsome antiques, and a replica of Penfield's invention—the iron-separating electromagnet—which ultimately led to the invention of the electric motor.

On the outskirts of Elizabethtown are the Meadowmount Music School, run by violinist Ivan Galamian for young virtuosi (who present highly professional recitals during the summer), and the Old Mill Art School, founded by the late Wayman Adams, whose portraits also grace the Adirondack Center Museum. These academies attract a more dignified class of tourists in the summer, setting Elizabethtown apart from the usual Adirondack souvenir-and-hamburger villages. Most Elizabethtown citizens are pleased with their lot, even if they don't receive as large a share of the summer tourist dollar. Just to the south, the resort town of Schroon Lake also gets a piece of the culture action as the primary site of the Adirondack–Champlain Music Festival, a sort of diminutive but polished Tanglewood.

These summer happenings can hardly be called innovations of native intellectual growth, since they are run by and meant for outsiders. But the modest museums spring from the people, and so does the unusual emphasis on schools and libraries. The recognition of education is

deeply felt and harks back to the makeshift classes held in eighteenth century pioneer cabins. Today, in spite of pernicious poverty and unemployment, Essex County spends almost as much money per pupil as the wealthy counties in the state. School taxes are high in every town but the complaints are not immoderately loud. Ambitious school consolidation plans are in various stages of development throughout the region, and it is a matter of some pride that a community college is in operation at Saranac Lake, the first and only college in the county. Few question the need for better education; the question most often heard is What will the young people do after their schooling is over?

The small but well-stocked libraries turn up in the most unlikely places. The hamlet of Upper Jay—consisting of a general store, a post office, a gunsmith shop, a garage, a deerskin crafts store, the Land of Make-believe theme park, a motel, a firehouse, and about sixty-five families in the best of times—also has its own Wells Memorial Library, staffed by a knowledgeable librarian and filled with a wide selection of books and magazines. It is the show place of the village and the citizens would as soon neglect their volunteer firehouse as their library.

Entertainment doesn't come easily in a depressed rural area, even with the advent of television in the North Country. A minor recreational event can sometimes take on the importance of a cultural happening. Even one as slight as a horseshoe-pitching tournament in the field be-

hind the school-bus garage reveals indigenous mores in a manner comparable, say, to the opening of Lincoln Center in New York City. Women are segregated from both the male participants and male spectators; raucous cheering for a good pitch is not permitted, even if the pitch was unexpectedly good; criticism is almost never uttered; celebration of victory is reserved and confined to a couple of beers after the contest; and dress is optional and rather varied.

Of course, there are the standard, more formal festivals, such as the Essex County Agricultural Fair, held every August at the Westport fairground, and the Fourth of July Celebration and Fire Department Benefit, on the Jay Village Green. The former event strictly adheres to American rural tradition, featuring 4-H Club displays, harness racing, thrill rides, a midway, band concerts, livestock judging, country and western music, demolition derbies, political hard sells, horse- and pony-pulling competitions, booths plugging everything from Hammond organs to Gideon Bibles, beery revelers, and shy farmers "just looking around." The annual Jay Fourth of July event stresses even hoarier traditions—stands selling home-cooked bean sandwiches and sugar cookies, the mouse game (in which bets are placed on what numbered hole a live field mouse will flee into when prodded with a stick), a greased-pole climb for a three-dollar prize nailed to the top, creaky fortune wheels, and fireworks at night. No ambulatory man, woman, or child would miss the fun, and since tourists are not particularly encouraged to attend, a typical

cross section of the native population at its ease can be observed. Most striking is the sameness of their physical appearance, regardless of ethnic ancestry. It is white America's melting pot come true. Bred out are the Italian eyes, the Irish complexion, the French hair, the English jaw, the Slavic cheekbones; what's left is a neutral amalgam, a new American race. The men are of a uniform heftiness. Their hair is close-cropped and straight, tending to early gray; their eyes are predominantly blue; their coloring is that of people used to being outdooors. They are contained, laconic, always proud, and sometimes embarrassed. The women invariably wear glasses, curl their short hair, look like good mothers but unattractive wives, and, although they dress and make up simply and neatly, they do little to hide signs of premature aging. They seem to be sisters or at least cousins, and more often than not they are. The children are blond, robust, bright, and more outgoing than their parents. The rare good time, the getting together, is quietly and fully appreciated.

At the infrequent ceremonious occasions, usually held in Elizabethtown, the members of the county establishment dress accordingly and display a more idiosyncratic physical appearance. Such an event was the dedication of the James N. Rosenberg Room at the Adirondack Center Museum. The late Mr. Rosenberg was an eminent lawyer and painter who, at eighty-one, still made his summer home near Elizabethtown. (He died on July 21, 1970.) He had become a revered fixture through the years of the Essex County scene and his paintings of the mountains,

and the people returned the compliment. On a hot August afternoon in 1968, the county's most distinguished citizens massed in their Sunday best to pay homage to their old friend. A few short speeches were delivered, neither making too much or too little of Mr. Rosenberg; the paintings were sincerely admired; cranberry-juice punch and homemade cakes were served; greetings and some gossip were exchanged; and everybody went home. It was an unsophisticated model for all similar ceremonies.

From the top of an Essex County mountain on a clear day, rolling stretches of the county unfold in startlingly fine focus, like a perfect relief map. In the constant, elevated perspective of the area, nature spookily imitates art: the lakes are like plastic sheets set in vivid molded verdure; the rivers are delicate silver ribbons; the rock faces and trees of other mountains seem too clearly visible for the distance, except those on the horizon, which are always a mysterious hazy blue; the villages and farms are flawless scaled-down representations, clean and white, disclosing nothing of the troubles within. Nature is a ubiquitous presence, whether the perspective is from a mountaintop or a village street. There is no escaping it. The people have long since become accustomed to living with nature; they are a part of it, married to it in a way that visitors from drearier topographies can never understand. It is their institution, their civilization, their art.

The seasons change with the sharpness expected of northeastern America, but the high Adirondacks and the

harsh Canadian winds lengthen the winters and abbreviate the summers. It can snow heavily in April, and in August a few maple leaves may suddenly turn after a nippy night. By late August, whole mountaintops can be gleaming red and yellow, even though the swimming is still comfortable in the lakes and rivers below. Spring and fall are dearly loved, winter is barely tolerated, and summer is mostly for making money. But, no matter what the season, weather is not just something to chat about; rather, it is ruminated upon, analyzed, tasted, collated, experienced, respected. Local radio and television stations give unusually frequent and complete weather reports, noting every possibility of change, and daily technical broadcasts from the Atmospheric Sciences Research Center, on Whiteface Mountain, are listened to as if they were divine decrees. A carefully planned budget can be devastated by a bad winter's fuel bills. Healthy crops are essential. An unseasonable frost or thaw can keep tourists away. Weather, then, means money. Yet there is room for country humor about the weather. Outdoor workers like to talk about its "heating up" when the temperature rises to ten below zero on a February afternoon. Children will tease any contemporary who covers his ears in winter or wears shoes in summer. Maxims for predicting the weather are cherished. (An Upper Jay matron, the late Mrs. Carrie Pelkey, once claimed that she had never missed with her rule of thumb: "If there's enough blue in the sky to make your husband a pair of pants, it'll be a good enough day.") It is no accident that the first thing a

visitor sees at the Adirondack Center Museum, in Elizabethtown, is a mammoth ground-to-roof "thermometer" attached to the building's exterior. It shows temperature records for the North Country; the lowest was fifty-two degrees below zero; the highest was a hundred and five above.

The region's flora and fauna are its cultural treasures, and the people are possessive and in awe of them. For instance, Dr. Orra A. Phelps, a retired physician in her mid-seventies, leaves her home near Saratoga every summer to take on the demanding post of ranger–naturalist for the Adirondack Mountain Club, which maintains a lodge and camping area eight miles outside Lake Placid, at the start of a trail to the peak of Mount Marcy. As an adviser on nature and ecology for the club's nearly six thousand members, she is constantly aware of even the most subtle changes in the North Country environment. "In the Adirondack forests, the floral growth and soil chemistry are just beginning to come back to what should be considered normal after the devastation of heavy lumbering and severe forest fires over the last hundred years," she said recently. "While there are very few places hereabouts where the giant spruce is undisturbed, the balsam fir and the white birch are slowly returning. The white pine, which was so sought after by the timber men, is having the devil's own time starting up again, because the seedlings don't like to be in the shade of bigger trees. They need the sun, but they don't grow fast enough to get ahead of the others. Our rare and beautiful Arctic

alpine plants, like the Lapland rosebay, are suffering from all the traffic up on the high peaks of Marcy, Haystack, and Skylight. There's a tightly woven mat of vegetation on top of those mountains, and the hikers and climbers sometimes carelessly walk on the plants and ruin their growth. We get as many as two hundred and fifty people on top of Mount Marcy on a summer weekend afternoon. We're trying to educate them to stay on the rocks and not on the rosebay. But in general the flora is holding its own, thanks to the tough Forest Preserve regulations. Oh, there's been a gradual diminution of wild flowers, though, and a few species may be lost entirely if the idea of a totally managed forest ever comes to pass. Witch-hobble and striped-maple shrubs, which our deer love to browse on, would certainly be trampled by lumbermen or cut out altogether to promote growth of timber trees."

The prevalent white-tailed deer of the Adirondacks have had a hard time of it during the past couple of winters, because of unusually deep snows. There are fewer deer now than there were twenty years ago largely because of winter starvation, Dr. Phelps believes, and not so much from the more mobile hunters and their high-powered rifles and telescopic sights. Moose and elk do not survive any longer in the Adirondacks; one theory has it that a parasitic disease carried by the whitetailed deer is particularly deadly for their bigger relatives. Panthers and wolves, too, are nonexistent now, but coyotes have been spotted from time to time near rabbit warrens. Bears flourish near outlying town dumps and isolated

camps, and martens and fishers have come back to the thickening woods. There are plenty of beavers, despite their profitable pelts. The beaver, however, is a source of ecological dispute. Streams are radically changed by beaver dams, and trees die in the backed-up pools. But local environmentalists like Dr. Phelps prefer the natural cycle of beaver dams and dead trees to open season on the North Country creatures. Besides, both native and hatchery trout favor the beaver pools over the clear, fast, generally insect-free streams, and everybody likes trout.

Herring gulls are still following the St. Lawrence to Lake Champlain and on up the rivers and streams to easy food, and most Adirondack avian varieties, from songbirds to hawks, are abundant. "The wild ducks never appreciated this area especially," Dr. Phelps said. "And we've had a report of only one raven seen in the last ten years. They seem to like Canadian forests better. One of the saddest things for me is the disappearance of the bald and golden eagles, those beautiful creatures that used to be all over these mountains. An occasional specimen comes to visit, but they haven't nested here recently. What happened was that through the years they ate fish full of DDT, which made their eggs too soft for the mother eagles to sit on. The only ones we ever see nowadays are the old, old birds who still have a sentimental feeling for our part of the world."

While a city dweller would consider a resident of an Essex village to be most certainly living in the country, the villager would disagree. The real country to him, if he

is solvent, is his camp, which can mean anything from a comfortable house to a tent erected in the wilderness. To go "up to camp" on a spring, summer, or fall weekend is to get away from it all and become reacquainted with one's cultural heritage. There in the woods, chipmunks are welcomed and tamed, healthy spruce and pine are admired, dying elms are pitied, trout are caught, venison is hung, flowers and vegetables are nursed, children are instructed, maple trees are tapped, and, as one camp owner put it, "you sit back and just eat the air with a spoon and don't let nothing get you down." The camp also satisfies the residual pioneer spirit in the North Country man. He feels closer to his ancestors there, and he likes the idea of making do with primitive means. Camps are frequently community projects, as pioneer cabins were two centuries ago. When a camp belonging to Jack Devlin, a Wilmington store owner, burned down, his friends pitched in and helped him rebuild it in a few weekends. All he had to pay for was the lumber. With snowmobiles catching on among those who can afford to buy them, camps can now be reached in the winter, and that season has thus been made a little more tolerable, if noisier. But the area's forests and wildlife are for everyone, rich or poor. "When you're in the woods, it's all different, whether you're hunting or fishing or sitting on your butt looking up at the trees," a seasonal restaurant worker said. "You forget about the rotten job you have, or maybe the job you don't have. Most of all, you forget about money and having to humble yourself taking a wel-

fare handout or food stamps. The time goes by in big chunks, and before you know it another day's gone and you feel better. It's like medicine for the soul, and it's a hell of a lot easier to take than religion."

Through its long history of ups and downs, the future of Essex County has been a matter of concern to inhabitants, but rarely of serious worry. Now there is worry in the county: worry about the dead and dying farms, the used-up mines, the mills that close, the clean-industry factories that never seem to open; worry about the tourists, the forests, the meat on the table, the long winters, the short summers; worry about the bills, the welfare, the job; worry about the children who are going away; and worry about the city's coming closer, and the consequent loss of uniqueness, of pride, of what's theirs. An old man who has lived along the western shore of Lake Champlain all his life explained the feelings of the people to a city friend not long ago. "All our problems are real ones, but nobody knows, nobody really cares," he said. "We're big and empty and poor—not like the Deep South but poor all the same. Mountain poor. The city people think of us—if they think of us at all—as a great big amusement park, a sort of woodsy Jones Beach, set up for their pleasure and whatever else they can take from us. Well, it's true, in a way. We have all this land, all this scenery, all this history. They see our nice clean houses and plenty of space for kids to run around in, and they think everything is peachy with us. Well, it isn't. We used to be able

to make do by ourselves, but it doesn't seem to work out that way anymore. Now we're in danger of disappearing altogether, like the old giant spruce. There are people living up here in the Sticks—not many, it's true, but people nevertheless—and we have the same wants and feelings as city people. Right now, like a lot of city people, we need some help."

AF521864